Jill

God bless you
in your meanwhile —
Be motherhood an
awesome exciting future! —

Enjoy!

Love from + Frank
S.O.S. 5.16

I have known Gail Ramsey for many years. In her quest for truth, fulfillment, and contentment, I have watched her as she stayed focused on one goal—the goal of knowing God in the most intimate way possible.

Through all the struggles of finding that "peace that passes all understanding," Gail has gained much wisdom through experience. She has now embarked upon a mission of sharing this wisdom in what I believe can be a life-changing book for many.

As you read *Dear God, It's Me Again*, you will see how God can bring you to victory in any situation of your life. You will find that His grace is sufficient.

May the Holy Spirit speak to you from each page as you search to know Him in a greater way.

—Darlene Bishop
Pastor of Solid Rock Church

Gail Ramsey is a gifted and compassionate teacher of God's Word. In *Dear God, It's Me Again*, she takes the hand of her reader and guides it gently into the hand of God, opening up His wisdom and truth with easy to read, down-to-earth advice. *Dear God, It's Me Again* is for anyone who desires to reach God's highest purpose for their life.

—Lana Corbi
Former President of FOX television
Former President of Hallmark television

A biblically based "How To" book on living in a hostile environment and dealing with life's traumas. From the depth and richness of her personal walk with God, Gail shares spiritual insights, understanding, and practical suggestions for living in today's fast-paced and turbulent world.

—Pat Matrisciana
President of Jeremiah Films

Dear God, It's Me Again is a collection of Holy-Spirit-inspired answers to the complex and sometimes hard to answer questions that we all have. Gail uses Bible references that confirm her hope-filled responses, giving the reader solid ground to stand on and some very real comfort and expectation from God.

Gail Ramsey's column is the biblically based "Dear Abbey" of the twenty-first century, unafraid to answer any of the contemporary problems and issues confronting people from all walks of life.

Jon Hanna
Former editor-in-chief of *Connection Magazine*

The timeless wisdom in *Dear God, It's Me Again* will surely speak faith and encouragement into many other lives. I am recommending this book to all who have accepted Jesus but do not yet know that they are joint-heirs with Jesus. It seems that I have heard more than enough sermons on our status as sinners, our need for repentance, our awesome responsibilities as Christians because of the awesome grace and mercy of God, and the sacrifices made by Christ; however, we don't hear enough about our rights, privileges, and authorities as Christians. This book will surely change that!

—Annie Tien
Web Producer
Author of *My Arguments with God*

Dear GOD
It's Me Again

GAIL RAMSEY

WHITAKER
HOUSE

DEAR GOD, IT'S ME AGAIN!

ISBN: 0-88368-430-6
Printed in the United States of America
© 2004 by Gail Ramsey

Women in Entertainment
8033 Sunset Blvd., Suite 221
Hollywood, CA 90046
www.womeninentertainment.org

Whitaker House
30 Hunt Valley Circle
New Kensington, PA 15068
www.whitakerhouse.com

Library of Congress Cataloging-in-Publication Data

Ramsey, Gail.
Dear God, it's me again / Gail Ramsey.
p. cm.
ISBN 0-88368-430-6 (hardcover : alk. paper)
1. Christian life. I. Title.
BV4501.3.R35 2004
242—dc22
2004018578

1 2 3 4 5 6 7 8 9 10   ⨂   10 09 08 07 06 05 04

DEDICATION

I dedicate this book to my son, Quinn, the joy of my life.

What a blessing God gave me in you! You are the perfect blend of strength and sensitivity, with a generous dash of humor thrown in just for fun. I know that you will pursue your dreams and fulfill your destiny.

In His love and mine,

Mom

Special Thanks

To Bob Whitaker Jr. for believing in me and for publishing this book.

To Pat Matrisciana, my champion and friend.

To my sister, Sue, for your daily encouragement as I wrote each chapter.

Darlene Bishop, thank you for being my rock. Surely no one has been through more trials than you have, yet you are always there, ready to listen and encourage with wisdom and love. You are not only my mentor, pastor, and friend...you are my hero.

CONTENTS

Introduction 9

1. Dear God, *Can We Talk?* 13

2. Faith, *Oh Me of Little!* 23

3. Purpose, *What on Earth Am I Doing Here?* 33

4. Favor, *Am I Special?* 43

5. Temptation, *Looks Good to the Eye!* 55

6. Love, *What Is It?* 63

7. Discouragement, *What Am I Doing Wrong?* 75

8. Anger, *Take It Away!* 85

9. Fear, *Your Greatest Enemy* 95

10. Peace, *Follow It!* 105

11. Envy, *Why Not Me?* 115

12. Forgiveness, *Do I Have To?* 123

13. Success, *You Were Born for It!* 131

14. Grace, *Where Can I Find Some?* 141

Conclusion 149

About the Author 153

INTRODUCTION

INTRODUCTION

E veryone who has ever lived has, at some point, taken a trip through the valley of hard times where it seems much easier to give up and quit than to go on. It's during these times, especially, that we cry out to God for help, knowing that we need hope beyond the scope of human limitations.

Dear God, It's Me Again provides answers drawn directly from the storehouse of timeless wisdom, giving you keys to succeed, whatever your need. It was designed to help you get through those difficult times victoriously. Each chapter of this book will give you instruction, compassion, and, now and then, even a good laugh. God hasn't failed anyone yet, and He's not going to start with you.

Your life CAN change! Your dreams CAN be accomplished! Your misery CAN be turned into victory! In *Dear God, It's Me Again* you will find encouragement and motivation to change your world...one chapter at a time. Read a few pages first thing in the morning to jump-start your day or any time you simply need a shot of encouragement. Share it with your friends who are dealing with their own issues. Remember, what you make happen for others, God will make happen for you.

INTRODUCTION

In this CNN (continually negative news) world that we are living in, it is vital that we renew our minds daily with something positive. *Dear God, It's Me Again* will help you to understand yourself and others better. It will enable you to grow closer to those you love and to motivate and connect with your children and friends. So take a minute, or ten—you deserve it! And as you read this book, one bite at a time, put the rest of your world on hold, and watch God turn your mess into a miracle. He's waiting for you.

The principles in this book are not new, but they are presented in a fresh way, which I hope will spur you on to go for the gold, reach beyond the limitations of your past, and grab hold of the success you were created to obtain: spiritually, physically, financially, and emotionally.

You are unique, and you are special. There is nobody else on the planet like you; but you are also not alone. As Oscar Wilde once said, "We are all in the gutter, but some of us are looking at the stars." Let this book help you by consulting the One who created them.

chapter one

DEAR GOD

Can We Talk?

Chapter One

DEAR GOD

Can We Talk?

Dear God,

My friend says that You often talk to her. Why don't I ever hear You talk to me? Is it really You speaking to her, or is she just imagining it?

T he question is not "Does God talk to us?" but "Do we take time to listen?"

We were born for fellowship with God. He longs for us to come away from our busy day and spend time with Him. He says, *"Come now, and let us reason together"* (Isaiah 1:18).

God is concerned with everything that concerns you. In fact, He knows the number of hairs on your head, as well as how many went down the shower drain this morning. If it matters to you, it matters to God.

God is *"no respecter of persons"* (Acts 10:34 KJV). What He does for one, He will do for another. The Bible says that God walked with Adam in the garden in the cool of the day. He talked with Moses and Jacob *"face to face"* (Genesis 32:30). He told Abraham He was going to make him the *"father of many nations"* (Genesis 17:4). He asked Noah to build an ark and gave him the blueprints to do it. God told Joseph the interpretation of Pharaoh's dream, which gave Joseph great favor with Pharaoh; within twenty-four hours, Joseph went from the prison to the palace and was made second in command over the entire nation. God wants to bless you the same way—or maybe with something greater and altogether new. The favor of God goes to those who make time for Him.

Believe it or not, God wants you to talk to Him even more than you desire Him to talk to you. He is jealous over you. He wants to be first in your life so He can bless you with all the wonderful things that He created with you in mind.

God wants you to talk to Him even more than you desire Him to talk to you.

In this hyperactive, zip-drive world, most of us "don't have time" to sit and talk with God, much less wait for Him to answer. Our schedules are jam-packed. But we make time to call a friend from our cell phone in the car, even if we're running late for another appointment, instead of using that time to talk to God. When we are overwhelmed, we should remember the following quote. Martin Luther said, "I have so much business I cannot get on without spending three hours daily in prayer." He understood the Source of his peace and power and knew that when things were overwhelming, he needed to go back to the One who made him for direction.

Far too often, when we're looking for answers, we settle for second best and consult our horoscope or dial a psychic, giving her our hard-earned money, hoping that she will wave a magic wand, give us pearls of wisdom, and make everything all right. The problem is, the psychic doesn't have the answers. She may make a lucky guess now and then, but she's operating through a familiar spirit, as opposed to the Spirit of truth, the Holy Spirit, the Spirit of God who knows all things.

In our supersonic attempt to be everything to everybody all the time, we have lost sight of who we really are. Most of us can hardly sit still to have our quiet time with God. We think that meditating on His Word is a "waste of time." But if people would take time to find peace and joy in the Lord, the world would be a better place. We can replace Prozac with God's peace.

God will never let you put Him in a box... He's too big!

God usually speaks in a still small voice, a voice so gentle that it's easy to ignore. It can't be heard in the midst of chaos. Take time to listen. The rewards are beyond description.

HOW DOES GOD SPEAK?

God speaks to you through His Word. He speaks to you through your circumstances. He may chose to speak to you, at times, through another person, a sermon, or a song. God says that He has placed enough in nature for us to get to know Him. God often speaks through dreams and visions, and sometimes through signs and wonders. God will never let you put Him in a box...He's too big! He will communicate to you when He wishes, as He wishes, however He wishes. He's God.

Most often, however, He will place a "knowing" down deep inside your spirit. It will be like a green light saying, "This is the way."

In 1995 I was invited to travel to Africa to help lead a crusade. The truth is, I really didn't want to go. It was too far away. I didn't have the finances. And, most importantly, who would watch my twelve-year-old son while I was gone? I fought the idea for months until one morning during prayer, God asked me, "How much money would you need for the trip?" I hadn't counted the cost because I had pretty much decided not to go. Out of obedience, and certain that when I did know the cost it would only confirm that this trip was out of the question and surely not God's will, I sat down at my desk and did the math.

Within a very short time, God provided, practically to the dollar, the amount I had calculated necessary for the trip. This certainly got my attention, but I still did not want to go. "Who will watch my son, Lord?" I asked. Within twenty-four hours, three people offered to care for my son while I was away. You would think that by this point I would have been convinced that this trip was, in fact, ordained by God, but still I resisted.

A few days later, as I wrestled with God in my prayer time, He convicted me of my rebellion. I broke down, repented, and asked His forgiveness. As always, He forgave me. Now, the problem was that I had procrastinated so long in my refusal to submit to His will that there was no longer enough time to get my visa before the departure date. I was short seven days. I had totally blown it.

I was really upset! Not only had I totally failed God in my refusal to walk according to His will for me, but I had lost the

opportunity to make things right! If only I had applied for the visa one week earlier, I would have been able to take the trip. I'd had four months to do it! I cried myself to sleep that night, filled with shame and remorse. God had always come through for me, and I had failed Him miserably.

At 5:45 a.m. the next morning, my phone rang. "Who on earth is calling me this early?" I wondered. Everyone who knows me knows that I'm a night person! The call was from Kenya, Africa. The pastor who had invited me to minister was extremely apologetic as he relayed the news that they would have to delay the crusade due to a legal issue. "Would it be possible for you to come one week later?" he asked me sheepishly. I have never felt closer to God than I did at that moment. Once again, He had moved on my behalf, giving me the seven days I needed...causing all things to work together for my good. "I'll be there," I told the pastor. Then I hung up the phone and rejoiced in the awesome presence of my wonderful and faithful Father, who loves me...in spite of my bad self.

My wonderful and faithful Father loves me... in spite of my bad self.

He had spoken to me through my circumstances. He had spoken to me in my prayer time. He had spoken to me through the actions of others and convicted me in my heart that it was, in fact, Him speaking. But there was one more message He had for me before He allowed me to board the plane for Africa.

As I sat alone at the airport gate—having arrived two hours early, just to be safe!—thanking God for all of His goodness and mercy toward me, I looked up and saw two huge angels standing in the corner. I had never seen angels like this! They stood about twelve to fourteen feet high, and somehow I

knew that they had been placed on assignment to protect me on this trip. "Wow, big angels!" I said, out loud. "Big assignment," answered a gentle voice back to me. It was a voice I knew well. He was with me again, blessing me again, speaking to me again...this time, using His angels.

HOW ELSE DOES GOD SPEAK?

The answer is, of course, however He wants to. He once spoke through a donkey, another time through a burning bush. Like I said earlier, God will not be put in a box. There are a few common ways, though, that He often communicates with His children. Here are some of them:

THE VOICE OF GOD

Rarely, God will speak to us audibly, as he did to Samuel. (See 1 Samuel 3:2–14.) Often God will put an idea on your heart or in your thoughts, and you will know that it was the voice of God, even though you didn't hear it with your ears. God speaks to your spirit.

God will often use conflict or problems to show us our progress, or lack thereof.

God sometimes speaks through other people. They may say, "God told me to share this with you," or they might not even realize they're giving you a sign from God. He can also speak through a program you catch on the radio or television, or a sermon that captures your situation perfectly.

CONFLICT OR PROBLEMS

God will often use conflict or problems to show us our progress, or lack thereof. When we are faced with confrontations, or

situations that push all of the wrong buttons, and we react according to old behavior patterns that we thought we had overcome, God reminds us, in a loving but firm manner, that we still have work to do in that particular area. Just like a good parent, *"Whom the* Lord *loves He chastens"* (Hebrews 12:6).

Each time we are "heated" by trials, we become more holy—if we allow God to work with us in the midst of the fire.

God can use the fires of adversity to shape us. Like a precious metal, each time we are "heated" by trials, we become stronger and purer, or more holy—if we allow God to work with us in the midst of the fire.

UNEXPECTED BLESSING AND FAVOR

Someone gives you a gift, or a promotion that you weren't expecting and says to you, "I don't know why, but I just felt led to give you this." Behind his or her words, you know it was God...just wanting to bless you. The smallest thing can be a touch from God—finding $20 you didn't know you had or getting an encouraging word from a friend or stranger.

ANSWERED PRAYER

You get the raise you've been praying for or the healing you've been standing in faith for, or that family member whose salvation you've been praying for finally accepts Christ. He's answered you by manifesting those specific things you've been asking Him for in prayer. Often the answers to our prayers are even abundantly more than we could have ever imagined or asked. (See Ephesians 3:20.)

RADAR

God has placed, deep inside each one of us, a built-in radar system. We refer to it as our *conscience*. Conscience is the eye of the soul. It guides us toward what we know to be right. We can follow it or reject it. Our decisions will determine our destiny.

Become sensitive to that small, still voice, and it will lead you to all success, joy, and righteousness. It will bring you those things your heart desires. Ignore it, and you will reap the harvest of disobedience. Pain, disappointment, and remorse will be your reward.

Our heavenly Father is a God of love who desires to give only the best to His children.

God has given us this awesome radar system to help us use our free will in positive ways that will ensure our blessing. It also warns us of danger or temptation. The best rule of thumb is this: When in doubt, don't. When you hear yourself asking, "Why not? Why shouldn't I do this?" you can be sure that your radar is on and working.

As we learn to spend time with God, walking and talking with Him through this journey called life, He will draw us to all good things—those things that bring joy, peace, abundance, and victory. Why? He is a God of love who desires to give only the best to His children. Our part is to stay in touch. It's hard for Him to guide us when we are not listening.

Prayer for Help

Dear God,

Forgive me for ever doubting Your presence. Help me to always remember that You're right beside me, just like You promised to be. Remind me, by Your Spirit, to take time each day to get away from the business, or "busy-ness," of my life and spend time alone with You.

Help me to run to You when I have a situation that seems overwhelming instead of running to the telephone to dump my problem on someone who can't help me the way You can.

I want to hear You speak to me, Lord. Help me to hear Your voice, whether it's through my conscience, my problems, or my circumstances.

Thank You for reminding me that You not only love me but that You really do want to be with me...alone. Thank You for all the prayers You have answered for me in the past and for the protection, provision, and favor You continue to pour upon my life.

Help me, Lord, to know You more. Amen.

Chapter Two

FAITH
Oh Me of Little!

Chapter Two

FAITH

Oh Me of Little!

Dear God!

Here I am, on my knees again! Why do I struggle so much? I used to be a person of great faith, then it somehow dissolved into little faith, and lately, I can't seem to find any faith at all! Help! Where did it go?

F aith is like a daisy. It needs encouragement in order to grow. A little sunshine, a little water, and it will flourish and bloom; but without proper care and nurturing, it will dry up and die.

If you're like many people, you've been the one with cheerleading faith for everybody: your mate, your children, your parents, and your friends. May I ask who's been there for you?

Some of us are like pitchers. We pour out into everybody's glass and forget to refill our own until, one day, we realize we're dying of thirst but, by then, the pitcher is empty.

FAITH'S CLOSE CALL WITH DEATH

When I first arrived in Hollywood several years ago, it seemed as though people were lining up to tell me about the odds of "making it" in show business. They strongly suggested I return home, get a "normal" job (whatever that means), and live happily ever after. I quickly realized that if I allowed myself to receive these words, my lifelong dream would be destroyed. My faith in my future, which I'd been envisioning from the age of ten, would die.

So, instead of listening to negative comments of death to my desires, I found some new friends who supported my dream and watered my daisy. We encouraged one another to "go for the gold!" We spoke words of success as we envisioned our victory. Faith and confidence grew and ushered us into our destinies.

Faith believes. Faith acts.
Faith never backs down.

Not much time passed before ABC was offering me a five-year contract to play a new leading role on their daytime soap opera, *General Hospital*. After five years with ABC, I went on to sign a two-year contract with NBC to star in a brand-new show called *Generations*, and later, I was blessed with another five-year contract by NBC for *California Dreams*.

Had I listened to the doubters and succumbed to the statistics, I would never have lived my dream. Faith believes. Faith acts. Faith never backs down.

Time to Grow Up!

Faith is a prerequisite for success. It is not complicated. It operates in the smallest child. A newborn cries, expecting someone to come and comfort, change, or feed her. Her faith and expectation of timely assistance will continue to grow until someone stops answering her cry. If the neglect continues, faith fades and expectation begins to die. Loneliness, sadness, even unworthiness may try to get a foothold in her little mind. If continued comfort and reassurance continue, however, her little mind grows big in faith, confidence, and security, knowing that without question she will always be taken care of.

We have a heavenly Father who will never leave us or forsake us.

As adults, we have (hopefully) learned to take care of ourselves. We have discovered how to feed ourselves with encouragement and clothe ourselves with confidence. We have also (hopefully) realized that we have a heavenly Father who will never leave us or forsake us. Our faith should grow along with our natural maturity. As we grow, we should have the knowledge and the experiences of our Father's love as proof to encourage our faith.

Faith That Survives

Abraham Lincoln, the sixteenth president of the United States, is an awesome example of a man of unfailing faith. He refused to be refused and denied to be denied.

At age twenty-two, Abraham Lincoln set up a business, but it failed. When he was twenty-three, he ran for legislature

and was defeated. Two years after failing in business, he tried again to set up another business...it also failed. Abe did not let any of these things discourage him. At age twenty-five, two years after being defeated in his run for legislature, he tried again. This time he was elected.

At the age of twenty-seven, after losing the love of his life, Abraham had a nervous breakdown. But, once again, he regrouped and began again to focus on his dreams. At thirty-four years old, he ran for Congress and failed. Three years later he tried again and succeeded. After serving for two years, he sought for reelection but was defeated. Abe still would not give up! At forty-six years old he decided to run for Senate...he was defeated. The following year, Abraham ran for a higher office, the office of vice president, and was defeated again.

We all have faith in something.

Most of us, at this point—had we ever reached this point!—would have thrown up our hands in defeat; but Abraham Lincoln, at fifty-one years of age, decided to go for the gold and run for president of the United States. He was elected and went on to become one of the greatest presidents America has ever had.

FAITH IS SIMPLE

Faith does not require a philosophical, homiletical, theological dissertation by a Greek scholar in order to be understood. Faith is simple. Faith the size of a mustard seed enables us to move mountains, the Bible says. (See Matthew 17:20.) Faith is resolute and unwavering. Faith is not moved by circumstances or the opinions of others.

We all have faith in something. If a snake crosses your path and you panic and scream, it doesn't mean that you have no faith. It simply means that you have more faith in the snake's power to harm you than in your own ability to run away or in God's ability to protect you.

Fear and faith cannot coexist. They are direct opposites. Faith is the absence of fear. We all must make a choice every day. Will we walk in faith, or will we walk in fear? Our decision will determine our thoughts. Our thoughts will determine our words. Our words determine our actions. Our actions create our character. And our character determines our destiny. Which will you choose: faith or fear?

We all must make a choice every day. Will we walk in faith, or will we walk in fear?

The faith of a child is honest, precious, and true. When my son was five years old, he loved going to Disneyland. Since we lived nearby, we visited the park often. One Sunday I promised him I would take him to Disneyland the following Friday. By Tuesday he had already put on his Mickey Mouse ears in anticipation of the great day ahead. He was excited and overflowing with expectancy of the fulfillment of that promise. He was already there in his little mind, enjoying the rides, the balloons, and the cotton candy. That's how we need to be as we wait on the promises of God and the manifestation of our dreams. *"So then faith comes by hearing, and hearing by the word of God"* (Romans 10 17). Expectancy is the breeding ground of miracles!

MIRROR, MIRROR, ON THE WALL

How do you see yourself? What is your vision? When you look in the mirror, who's looking back? Our self-image is vitally important to our success and far more powerful than

28

our circumstances. The way we see ourselves is crucial to our lives. The Bible says it this way: *"As* [a man] *thinks in his heart, so is he"* (Proverbs 23:7). My college mentor had another version of the same truth: "If you think you can, or if you think you can't...you're right." So, what do you think?

If we don't have a vision of our desired destination, it's a sure fact that we'll never arrive there. Many people just "wait and see what tomorrow brings." They simply accept their lot in life without ever trying to change their circumstances. They're complaining instead of creating; groveling instead of growing; existing instead of excelling.

If you think you can, or if you think you can't...you're right.

We were not created simply to take up space on this planet. We were created in the image of our Father, the ultimate Creator. In other words, we were created to create! "What am I supposed to create?" you ask. What excites you? What are your gifts? What are your talents? What makes your heart smile? What would you choose to do if you knew that you could not possibly fail? That is what you are supposed to create. "But that seems impossible! I don't have the talent, resources, connections, or brains to make that happen!" Good. If it seems impossible, that doesn't mean it's not your destiny. It just means that you'll need to rely on God to bring it to pass.

ALL THINGS ARE POSSIBLE

Good ideas are easy to find. *God* ideas can be terrifying because you know that it's going to take a miracle. Thomas Edison, with a vision to create something that had never before existed, experienced a multitude of failures before he

was able to say, "Let there be light," and it was. He refused to be defeated! His faith in his vision grew stronger with each defeat.

If it seems impossible, it just means that you need God to bring it to pass.

Babe Ruth struck out 1,330 times. That's almost twice as many times as he hit home runs. Henry Ford had a vision that automobiles could be mass-produced. Nobody else believed it was possible. But Henry said, "None of this! Put it on the line. Let every man screw in a screw, and we'll make it cheap." Not only did he see his vision manifested, but before he died, nearly every family in the United States had an automobile. By the end of his days here on earth, Henry Ford was worth over a billion dollars...all because of a vision and a decision to walk in faith.

Faith can put you on a road where you can do things you've never done before. Things you only imagined or caught glimpses of in movies can begin to take root in your mind and give you visions and ideas meant just for you to create. Nobody else on this planet has your fingerprints. Nobody else will be able to bring to pass that thing you were born to do. Others may try, but they will never do it the way you could have done it had you stepped out in faith... because it's your destiny.

It's time to get out of the boat, step out of the box, put your eyes on the prize, and go for it! God wants us to become people of faith so that, when it comes to the great emergencies of life, we won't have to depend upon our brains, our bank accounts, or the dispatcher at 911. Only believe, only believe. All things are possible. Only believe!

Prayer for Faith

Dear God,

Make me a person of great faith. Help me to see my potential. Quiet my anxieties about tomorrow. Remove my doubts. Give me a vision of victory to help me accomplish those things I was born to achieve.

Fill me to be a fountain. Use me to be a vessel. Train me to be triumphant in everything I do. Help me to see myself the way You see me—as an overcomer, as more than a conqueror, as the apple of Your eye!

Give me wisdom, boldness, courage to change those things that need changing, and faith to follow through to the end. Amen.

Chapter Three

PURPOSE

What on Earth Am I Doing Here?

Chapter Three

PURPOSE
What on Earth Am I Doing Here?

Dear God!

What on earth am I here for? Do I have a purpose?

How can I discover my destiny?

U ntil you can answer those questions, your life will be filled with emptiness; your self-worth and self-esteem will disintegrate. But here's the good news and the bottom line: There is a purpose for your life. (See Psalm 20:4.) There is a specific God-given destiny planned for you alone— an awesome, glorious, fulfilling life of joy with your name on it. (See Jeremiah 29:11.)

In the eyes of men, you may have been an accident, but in the eyes of your Creator, you are perfectly and *"wonderfully made"* (Psalm 139:14). You were planned, wanted, prepared, and predestined for such a time as this.

34

There is a type of eel in Germany that leaves the Rhine River and travels three thousand miles through the Atlantic Ocean. When she arrives off the coast of Cuba, she deposits her eggs, and then she returns to her native waters in Germany. The young eels grow up in these Cuban waters. Once they're grown, they return to their mother, three thousand miles away...divine guidance!

If the fish and the birds can figure out what they're intended to do, we can also live and move in our destiny.

More evidence of divine guidance is the Arctic bird that flies by astronomy and migrates twenty-two thousand miles each year, from the Arctic to the Antarctic.

Surely if the fish and the birds can figure out where they're going and do what they were intended to do, then we, the only species with a soul, can also live and move in our destiny. God has made us in His own image. Divine guidance is our heritage!

WHERE DO I START?

Erase the board and start from scratch. What makes you smile? What are you good at? What do others think you're good at? What areas have you had success in? The Bible tells us that *"a man's gift makes room for him"* (Proverbs 18:16).

One day, during my second year of working on ABC's *General Hospital*, I was bored to tears and frustrated beyond my capacity to endure. At the time, my character, "Susan Moore," did not have much of a storyline, and I was only shooting one or two days a week, yet I was bound by a contract that prevented me from working on any other show. Although I

loved my job, I needed more of a creative outlet than one day a week provided.

I began pacing back and forth in my dressing room at the studio, asking myself out loud, "Okay, what can I do? What am I good at? What else do I know? Where is a need that I could fill? And how can I do that 'something else' while still remaining faithful to my contract with ABC?" It was perplexing at first, but as I started to force myself to come up with ideas based on my gifts, talents, and interests, suddenly it was as if a light was turned on in my mind. "I know!" I said to myself out loud. "I know about health and fitness and eating the right foods! Maybe I could write a column on health, and feature Hollywood stars...I could call it *Healthy in Hollywood*!"

Ask yourself, "What can I do? What am I good at? Where is a need I could fill?"

The negative side of me, or the devil, as some would say, began immediately to discount and dismiss my idea as "ridiculous." "Every magazine already has a column on health" it argued. "Besides, you've never written a column. You wouldn't know how."

My desperation to find a creative outlet overpowered the negative gunfire aimed at my mind. I went to the coffee table in my dressing room, picked up my magazines, and began to scan them for columns on health. Within moments I had found that although most magazines did in fact have health columns, the soap opera magazines did not! I was bubbling over with joy, confidence, and total faith that this was "it."

Immediately, I thought about the editor of the most popular daytime magazine, a woman who had interviewed me for several past articles. I had her number and decided to call.

Before I picked up the phone, however, I had a conversation with her in my mind, discussing my idea for *Healthy in Hollywood*, a new column for her magazine. In my imagination, she said, "Yes," and was thrilled with the idea, of course. I quickly dialed the phone, not wanting to give fear a chance to get a foothold. She was on the line within seconds, and I began my pitch just as I had rehearsed it moments earlier in my mind.

In those few short seconds, my life was changed. The editor not only said "yes," as she had in my imaginary conversation, but she was so excited about the idea that she asked me if I could get the first column to her within two weeks. "Sure," I said happily, then I hung up the phone. After a few short moments of bliss, I was bombarded with questions of doubt. "You've never written anything in your life! Are you crazy? Now what are you going to do? You'll never pull this off! You're going to look like an idiot!" I instantly reminded myself that I *had* written something before...I had written lots of term papers in college, and I'd had a job writing continuity at a local television station one summer. As the Bible says, *"I can do all things through Christ who strengthens me"* (Philippians 4:13). I could do this, and I would!

I did. Within a few short months, my new column, *Healthy in Hollywood*, was expanded into a two-page regular article, featuring everyone from Richard Dean Anderson to Richard Simmons. My editor was pleased, and my creative void, filled. Two years later, I had to stop writing *Healthy in Hollywood* due to a major storyline change for my character on *General Hospital*. I began shooting five days nearly every week (God is good!) until I fulfilled my contract and left the show.

Why am I telling you all this? To encourage you and remind you that *"with God all things are possible"* (Matthew

19:26) and that you too have a "column" inside of you; you just have to become desperate enough to find it. So, where do you start? You start right where you are. God says that when we're faithful over the little things, He'll make us master over bigger things. (See Luke 19:17.)

GIVE ME A CLUE

Sometimes, the thing that angers us the most can be tied to our purpose. My former teacher, mentor, and spiritual covering, Dr. Lester Sumrall, was angered by the number of God's children in the world who didn't have enough food to eat. His anger at this atrocious injustice drove him to develop his *Feed the Hungry* program in 1987.

The thing that you are passionate about could be tied to your purpose.

Dr. Sumrall was a wise and compassionate man who operated in powerful authority. He was not interested in amassing great wealth but determined to share the bounty of the world with those in need. He was passionate about his mission and set out to accomplish his vision with fierce faith and supernatural boldness. His dream not only became a reality but far surpassed his original vision. Dr. Sumrall's *Feed the Hungry* program has given millions of dollars in food and supplies to people around the globe. As he so often said, "This is just the beginning." When he died on April 29, 1996, he passed the baton to the next generation. His sons continue the mission.

Michael J. Fox, one of the most beloved television stars of all time, is angry at Parkinson's disease and the destruction it causes. He is adamant about helping to find a cure. For right now, that's his purpose, and he's passionate about it. Because

of his determination to help destroy this disease, many have been given new hope; and millions of dollars have "miraculously" appeared for research.

The Amber Alert is another wonderful thing that came out of a personal disaster. This system allows police to alert local communities to be on the lookout for missing children as soon as they suspect the child is in danger. Through the emergency broadcasting system and the media, millions of people can be on the lookout almost immediately for the kidnapper's vehicle and the child. Across the country, Amber Alert Plans are credited with helping safely recover children.

Children are being rescued all across the country because somebody was bold enough to say, "No more! You won't take our children!"

There is joy, peace, and great satisfaction that comes from stepping out in faith and accomplishing your purpose.

GO WITH THE FLOW

Your purpose in life should not have to be conjured up. It should flow like a river out of your innermost being. Your purpose, or destiny, can be distinguished from other ideas by the fact that it never leaves you. It will simply "feel right"... like the right size shoe as opposed to one that's a size too small.

Your purpose in life should flow like a river out of your innermost being.

Follow the peace! Just because your father was a doctor, and his father was a doctor, doesn't necessarily mean that your purpose in life is to be a doctor. You may have been created to

39

be an artist, a mortician, or an apprentice to Donald Trump! What feels right to you *inside?* What makes your spirit leap inside your belly and say, "Yes! That's it!"?

Life is like a multiple-choice test, but there are no wrong answers. Follow your heart!

When my son entered college, he was forced to put down a major and minor for his study plan. He was very torn between molecular genetics and theatre, and he was extremely gifted in both. He eventually decided to go with a double major and pursue both fields until he had more clarity. After his second year, he knew without question that acting was where he belonged. As a parent who wants security for her child, I had hoped he would continue in medicine; but as an actor who totally understood his heart, I was forced to support him with joy (and many prayers!).

Beware of accepting your world the way it is unless you want to live in it for the rest of your life. That which you tolerate, you will keep.

Throw off the limits! Get desperate! Who would have thought that Beethoven would continue to write beautiful music even after he became totally deaf? Or that Franklin D. Roosevelt could become president of the United States in spite of being confined to a wheelchair? You were born a winner! Don't die a loser.

Prayer for Purpose

Dear God,

Please help me to be all that I was created to be. Help me to see myself through Your eyes and to know that You care for me. Help me to get rid of the negative image I see in the mirror and replace it with the winner You meant me to be.

Show me my purpose. Define my destiny. Surround me with positive people who will see the potential You've placed in me and encourage me to develop it. Help me to be bold enough to step out of my comfort zone and enter my promised land. Amen.

Chapter Four

FAVOR

Am I Special?

FAVOR

Am I Special?

Dear God!

Why do I always feel like the least of the least?

Everyone I know seems to be better than me. I want people

to like me and to think that I'm special. Is that wrong?

I t's not wrong to want to feel special. You were born special! So special, in fact, that nobody else in the entire world has your fingerprints! Many people, however, have a low self-image due to negative childhood experiences, bad marriages, or simply as a result of not having the love and support we all need in order to feel loveable and "special." These people often become introverted and live in a world of sadness, anger, or frustration.

The truth is, God doesn't play favorites. (See Acts 10:34.) We are all His children, and He does not love one more than another. As we begin to see ourselves through His eyes, we will realize that He wants only the very best for us. As we realize that each one of us is the *"apple of His eye"* (Deuteronomy 32:10), we can begin to create new, positive images of ourselves in our own minds. God's opinion of us makes man's opinion irrelevant!

God's opinion of us makes man's opinion irrelevant.

DEALT A BAD HAND?

As a child, Adolf Hitler was regularly beaten by his father, Alois. His parents both died while he was a teenager, leaving him to live as an orphan for six years. His dream as a young boy was to enter the priesthood, a dream that never came to pass. Most of us know the end of his story.

Hitler's contemporary, Joseph Stalin, was also beaten continually by his drunken father, who eventually abandoned him and his mother. Stalin contracted smallpox at the age of six, which scarred his face for life. Stalin was a bright student and had the same dream that Hitler had—to become a priest.

Stalin entered a religious seminary in 1894 to study for the priesthood in the Georgian Orthodox Church. It was here that he became interested in the theories of Karl Marx, the German social philosopher. He joined a secret Marxist revolutionary group in 1898 and was expelled from the seminary in 1899 for his involvement. Stalin was arrested and exiled many times. Between 1907 and 1917, he spent seven years in prison.

He soon became the leader of the Russian Communist Party and was dictator by his fiftieth birthday.

Stalin had millions of peasants killed for their refusal to obey him. He ruled by terror—and in 1935 he started a "purge" (elimination) of the old Bolsheviks. He killed anyone who might have threatened his power and even executed thousands of his own Communist Party members, leaving no one to oppose his policies.

Hurting people hurt people. Have you been hurt? Have you been healed?

Can you see by these two examples how we can be affected by our early treatment as children? Can you see the similarities of these two young boys and how they cried out for love under the guise of wanting to enter the priesthood? "Maybe somewhere, someone would love me. Maybe somewhere, there is a God who cares." I wonder how many times they cried themselves to sleep as small children, hoping these thoughts would be true. Unfortunately for them, and millions of others whose lives were destroyed by them, they never had their minds renewed with the truth, which is that there is indeed a God who loved them, who wanted to protect them and surround them with favor. A God who promises us in His Word that even though our father and mother may forsake us, He will always take care of us. (See Psalm 27:10.)

Hurting people hurt people. Have you been hurt? Have you been healed?

CHANGE THE TAPE

Don't let your past determine your future! You can't change your past, but you can create your future. By replacing

the old, negative, condemning thoughts that you used to have about yourself with new, positive, encouraging thoughts. You can recreate your life into whatever you want it to be. You can feel special—because you are!

It begins with a new image in your mind, an "extreme makeover" for some of us. Just as a beautiful new building cannot be built until the architect designs the plans, so you must begin to visualize what you want your life to look like. The Bible says it this way: *"As* [a man] *thinks in his heart, so is he"* (Proverbs 23:7). You may say, "Well, my life looks pretty good except for my finances." Then simply begin to see yourself with plenty of money, out of debt, and with lots left over to help others. Begin to think yourself wealthy, because "as a man thinks," so he becomes.

Your second step to developing your new image is to watch your mouth! You will have what you say. (See Mark 11:23.) Did you ever wonder why some people are always sick? No matter how many times they go to see a doctor, they still remain sick. Maybe it's because all they ever talk about is how sick they are! *"Death and life are in the power of the tongue"* (Proverbs 18:21). You have the power to change your world by the things you believe and the words you speak. Speak life to the good and death to the bad.

What does this have to do with favor? I'm so glad you asked. *Favor* is the hand of God at work in your life. Favor can do for you in a day what you couldn't do for yourself in a lifetime. Favor will change your insecurity into self-confidence.

HOW DO I GET IT?

You will reap what you sow. Expect good things to happen, and those will be the things that start happening

to you. Your life flows in the direction of your most dominant thoughts, good or bad. Discipline your mind to think only good thoughts, and expect only good things to happen. Expectancy is the breeding ground of miracles! Your mind is the drawing board of tomorrow's circumstances. Your thoughts are the beginning of your reality. Replace thoughts of lack, sickness, and inferiority with positive thoughts of abundance, health, and confidence. The way you see yourself will usually be the way others see you. If you don't view yourself as successful, kind, and worthy, why should anyone else?

Favor is the hand of God at work in your life.

Imagine yourself as highly favored in every area of your life. Imagine yourself as the son or daughter of the King. There is nothing you desire that you can't have. Others look up to you, and you are kind to them, returning the favor. God has crowned you *"with glory and honor"* (Hebrews 2:7). The world is at your fingertips because your father, the King, owns everything! All the silver and gold belong to Him. (See Haggai 2:8.) His word is the final word, and when He speaks, people tremble. When He commands a thing, it is done, and you are the apple of His eye.

Here's another sure way to quick-start favor flowing into your life. Begin to show favor to others. Remember, you reap what you sow.

The Bible tells us that what we make happen for others, God will make happen for us. *"Whatever good anyone does, he will receive the same from the Lord"* (Ephesians 6:8). As you begin to walk in a new appreciation for others and for yourself, you

will be amazed at the favor that will begin to pour out into your life.

Expect miracles to unfold before you today. Get excited! Plan your victory party! God loves you! He favors you! Favor flows to you from every direction. You are blessed beyond anything you've ever imagined! (See 1 Corinthians 2:9.)

Make a decision to never again confess (speak out loud) your negatives. Confess that you are a success and that nothing is impossible. Confess that you like people and that they like you. Expect favor with people in every situation. Have a positive attitude toward every situation you encounter, even the bad ones. Expect them to turn around because of the favor God has given you. Don't accept failure and defeat because, after all, your father is the King! He will work all things out for your good. (See Romans 8:28.)

WILL THIS REALLY WORK?

What have you got to lose? If what you have been doing had worked, then you wouldn't be feeling that you were the "least of the least" and that everyone else was better than you. If you want things to be different, then you are going to have to do things differently. I can personally guarantee that this worked for me.

I used to feel very much like you do, the "least of the least," and totally unloved. Because of this mind-set, which had evolved from a lack of love and nurturing as a child, I withdrew from people and developed a chip on my shoulder. They didn't like me, so I wouldn't like them either. Needless to say, it was a pretty miserable existence.

The summer after eighth grade, I got the following revelation: In three months, I would be entering a new high school

across town. Nobody would know me there. If I just pretended that I was popular, how would they know that I wasn't? This revelation took me into what I like to call the "fourth dimension." I began to see myself as I wanted to be, instead of the way I had been in the past. I was tired of not having friends, and of being the weird girl that nobody liked. I wanted to be popular, special.

I spent that entire summer visualizing myself in my new role as "the popular girl." I continually tried to imagine what it would feel like having everyone wanting to be my friend and having favor surround me. It was fun, creating this new picture in my mind, and I was determined to make it my new reality.

We can change our destiny by changing our thoughts.

Fortunately, because I had no friends with which to share my newfound revelation, there was nobody to rain on my parade and speak death to my new dream. (When you begin to plant seeds of favor into your life, it is imperative that you don't allow those who won't support you to discourage you. This may mean not discussing your plans with everyone.)

When September arrived, I was ready, and I boarded the school bus as "the popular girl." I put on a big smile and all the confidence I could gather as I walked to my seat. By the time we arrived at school, I had made at least seven or eight new "best friends." Later that same day, I was nominated by my new classmates to be class president. I had arrived! Finally, somebody liked me. I was special. It felt great!

I learned through this experience that, in order to have friends, I first had to be a friend. I also realized that we can

change our destiny by changing our thoughts. We don't have to remain stuck in a rut. We have the power to step out into that fourth dimension and create a new reality. It all begins inside. We can see ourselves as losers, or winners—it's totally up to us. By the way, I made cheerleading squad that first year and was voted "Sweetheart Queen" as a sophomore. Junior year was the best, as I became captain of the cheerleaders and dated the captain of our basketball team. In my senior year, the entire school elected me as secretary of the student council. Favor surrounded me. All things were possible! My life had been changed forever.

In case you're thinking, "Well, that was just a fluke. Real life isn't like high school," let's fast-forward to Hollywood, California, 1992.

A friend from my church called to ask me if I would come in and audition for *California Dreams,* a new sitcom he was going to be directing for NBC. The truth is, at this point, I wanted to leave Los Angeles; but, out of respect for my friend, I said yes. I figured they probably wouldn't cast me anyway because I'd never done comedy.

When I arrived at the audition, I found the room filled with tall blonde actresses. Being barely 5' 4" and brunette, I definitely didn't fit in. Two days later, I got a callback for a second audition. I figured they were just being polite to my friend by including me. When I returned to NBC, it was the same story—a room full of tall blondes...and me. The next day, I received another invitation for a third callback. I began to wonder if God was up to something.

By the time I returned home after the third audition, my agent had already left a message on my answering service saying that NBC wanted me to come back, with the possibility

51

of a five-year contract, and read for the network as they made their final selection. I went. They had narrowed it down to three: two tall blondes, and me. When the audition was over, the director called me into his office to inform me that he had never before seen a room full of network executives agree on anything; but they had chosen me, unanimously. Immediately, I heard God speak, "When I have a plan for your life, I will turn the very hearts of men toward you, and give you favor." I replied, "God, I know it was you...because I don't do comedy."

God's plan is always better than our own.

God's plan is always better than our own. I had more fun working on *California Dreams* than on any other show I had previously been a part of. Favor is better than money. Money can't buy you favor, but favor can bring you money.

Prayer for Favor

Dear God,

Please help me to walk in favor. Help me to always see the glass half full instead of half empty. Help me to trust You more, and to remember that I'm special and that You love me more than I love myself.

Show me my life filled with Your favor, and help me to hold fast to that vision. Give me the courage to step out in faith and create those things in my life that would be a blessing to me and to others.

Help me to show favor to others, so that they, too, might begin to see themselves as special. Thank You for reminding me that, with You, all things are possible. Amen.

Chapter Five

TEMPTATION

Looks Good to the Eye!

TEMPTATION

Looks Good to the Eye!

Dear God,

I've been dating this guy who is absolutely wonderful! He's handsome, funny, and he even sings to me! He thinks I'm beautiful. I want to move ahead in this relationship, but how can I know for sure that he's the one I should marry?

My parents are concerned because he doesn't have a job, but they don't know him like I do, and they don't understand how he makes me feel.

Help! What should I do?

TEMPTATION

Wisdom always waits. Whenever there is a question in your mind, or a check in your spirit about anything, the best advice is, When in doubt, don't.

This man may have been sent straight from heaven, but he could also be a fatal distraction sent from the opposite direction. Temptation always looks good to the eye. If it weren't so attractive, it wouldn't be so hard to resist. Sometimes it even comes disguised as a knight in shining armor.

> Temptation always looks good to the eye.
> If it weren't so attractive, it wouldn't
> be so hard to resist.

Before we throw this man out the window, however, let's take a look at the facts. And, before we even do that, let me say this: *"In the multitude of counselors there is safety"* (Proverbs 11:14), so it was wise for you to talk with your parents, people who know you and love you, and to get their advice. Whether you agree with them or not regarding this current relationship, you know that they have your best interests at heart. You'll have more information with which to make your decision—besides, they might be right.

Okay, here we go. First of all, feelings are fickle. They change like the seasons. Basing any life decision on your feelings is setting yourself up for certain disaster. Second, he doesn't have a job. What are you thinking? When there's no food to eat and you're hungry, those love songs and sweet words about your beauty are not going to do it for you. Third, if and when he doesn't live up to the image you now have of him as this handsome, wonderful, good knight who loves, protects, and provides for you, your respect for him as a man will fly right out the window—followed closely by your desire

for physical intimacy (sex). Once that goes, the honeymoon is over.

Now let's look at the bright side! If he is as wonderful as you believe him to be, then he won't mind waiting until he can provide some security for you before he asks you to be his wife. He will also give you a ring, will have a steady job, and will provide a place for you to live—as opposed to moving into your apartment, eating your food, driving your car, and playing your CDs. You are worth the wait!

Temptation promises you the rainbow but gives you the rain.

Temptation promises you the rainbow but gives you the rain. It comes in many colors, shapes, and disguises. I'm not giving you this advice off the top of my head. I lived the lesson....

BLUE EYES AND BLUE JEANS

After having been a single mother for eighteen years, it was very flattering to have a certain young, extremely handsome man begin to pursue me. He had the bluest eyes and the blondest hair I'd ever seen. Just my type! He was also a very talented and anointed musician and worship leader. As if this weren't enough, he loved God and came from a wonderful family made up of four generations of preachers. Had I struck gold or what? But, in spite of all the pluses, I had a minus in my spirit...a red flag was waving.

For six months after our first meeting, I refused to go out with him. I was concerned with the difference, not only in our ages but also in our life experiences and, even more

importantly, our commitment levels to God. I had made a huge commitment ten years earlier. It included everything.

My spirit was willing, but my flesh was growing weaker by the day. He had a smile that could melt steel, and he was crazy about me. I finally agreed to spend some time with him. It was fun. He made me laugh (something I had never spent much time doing). He took me home to meet his parents and grandparents. They were wonderful and warmly welcomed me as if I were part of the family. They were also in complete agreement that he and I were a great match, perfect for one another.

I met one-on-one with his mother, who listened to all my concerns and then said simply, "Gail, all I see are two people who belong together." But I still had that red flag waving deep down inside of me. I began to second-guess myself. "Maybe this is my problem," I thought, "They can't all be wrong... can they? Could this just be my own fear of intimacy? Is this God at work in my life, or is this a fatal distraction that could destroy my destiny?" I just wasn't sure.

I won't tell you how my dilemma ended, but I will tell you this: I wish there had been someone back then whom I respected and trusted to sit me down and, lovingly but firmly, tell me some of the things I've just told you. It would have saved me a lot of time and anguish...that is, if I had been willing to listen.

He may be a perfectly wonderful man, but he may not be right for you...or he may not be right for now. Being out of God's timing is just as detrimental as being out of His will. *"To everything there is a season, a time for every purpose"* (Ecclesiastes 3:1).

Don't compromise! Heed the red flags. They are there for a reason. And, most importantly, follow the peace! *"You will*

keep him in perfect peace, whose mind is stayed on You" (Isaiah 26:3). When God is in your situation, there is peace in your heart.

THE COLOR OF MONEY

As I said earlier, temptation comes in many colors. The color green has taken many captive, not just through jealousy, but through greed. We need only look to the news and its big stories of Enron, WorldCom, or Martha Stewart. Does no one have morals anymore?

Right is still right if nobody's doing it. Wrong is still wrong if everybody's doing it.

Temptation begins with a look, "Look at how much money I could make!" Followed by a thought, "Hmm, if I just move the numbers around a little, nobody will ever notice." Culminating in an action, "Okay, I'm going to do this quickly, before anyone sees me. It's no big deal. After all, everyone else is doing it." Before you realize it, you've been caught like a fly in a spider web—and destroyed.

Right is still right even if nobody's doing it. Wrong is wrong even if everybody's doing it.

How many have given in to the lure of the dollar? How many have succumbed to the seduction of power? Power brings money. Money brings power. The two are like Siamese-twin serpents, waiting to destroy you then swallow you alive.

There is nothing wrong with money in and of itself. In fact, money is a good thing. The Bible says that *"money is the answer for everything"* (Ecclesiastes 10:19 NIV), and that *"it is* [God] *who gives you the power to get wealth"* (Deuteronomy 8:18).

But God also says that *"the silver is Mine, and the gold is Mine"* (Haggai 2:8). He encourages us to *"seek first the kingdom of God"* and says that if we do, *"all these* [other] *things shall be added to you"* (Matthew 6:33), for He *"delights in prosperity of His servant"* (Psalm 35:27 NASB).

So God doesn't care how much money you have, as long as what you have doesn't have you! The Bible says, *"I pray that you may prosper in all things and be in health"* (3 John 2). But it also says that *"the love of money is the root of all evil"* (1 Timothy 6:10 KJV). It's all about getting our priorities straight.

Let's take a look at two people, a husband and wife, who were so full of greed and so afraid of lack that they lied about their profits on a sale. Their names were Ananias and Sapphira. You can find them in the fifth chapter of the book of Acts. When their dishonesty was revealed, it was pointed out to them that they had not only stolen from men, but from God. Upon hearing these words, they both fell dead. The Bible tells us, *"The wages of sin is death"* (Romans 6:23).

Most people today, however, do not simply fall dead when their sin (be it stealing, adultery, child abuse, or murder) is exposed. They usually hire the best attorney they can find, look for a loophole to squeeze through, then go back to their business, and live the way they choose. But even if they escape jail time, they are paying with their eternal soul. So much for progress in our civilized world.

Temptation is not your friend.

Prayer for Strength

Dear God,

Please help me to walk away when temptation draws near. Help me to see it before it takes my hand and leads me in the wrong direction. Make me strong when I feel weak, and give me courage to do the right thing. Please forgive my past mistakes, and give me a brand new start.

Make me like You, Lord, honest and true in everything I do. Remind me that the plans You have for me are far better than any I could create for myself. Amen.

Chapter Six

LOVE

What Is It?

Chapter Six

LOVE
What Is It?

Dear God,

How can I know if it's really love? Is it possible for love to last? My father abandoned me at three, and since then, all of my relationships have ended badly. Is there any hope of true love for me?

F ew people ever get outside of themselves long enough to understand and know what love really means. Many women think of love in terms of what they will receive when they meet "Mr. Right," as opposed to what they will be able to give him when he arrives. Love is giving. Love is putting another's needs above our own. It's been said that a mother's love for her child is the closest thing to unconditional love that a human being can experience. Love is the glue that holds marriages together.

Love is not a feeling, but a choice. God is love, and His love is unconditional. God loved the world so much *"that He gave His only begotten Son"* (John 3:16). Love gives. Sometimes love is tested and becomes difficult to hold on to, but *"love never fails"* (1 Corinthians 13:8). Love shifts our focus from ourselves to others and helps them become the very best they were created to be. When we love others, we truly delight in their successes, their accomplishments, and their growth. There is no jealousy or envy. We rejoice in their victories as if they were our own. Love is about giving.

> Love shifts our focus from ourselves to others and helps them become the very best they were created to be.

Money can buy lots of things, but it can't buy love. Power can seduce and motivate, but it cannot buy love. Neither your MD, your PhD, nor your IQ will determine how much love you receive, any more than it will determine how well you will handle love once you do receive it. The only way to get love is to first give love. "You reap what you sow" (see Galatians 6:7), and the only way to keep love is to keep on loving.

GIVE ME AN EXAMPLE

One of the greatest advocates and examples of love, in my opinion, was Mother Teresa. She continually reminded us all to "love your neighbor." She lived nearly ninety years and was the personification of compassion. She ministered to the poorest of the poor in Calcutta and called herself "God's pencil," describing herself as "a tiny bit of pencil with which He writes what He likes."

I had the honor of meeting Mother Teresa in Washington, D.C., in 1994, where she was the keynote speaker at the President's prayer breakfast. It was an experience I will never forget. This tiny, frail woman had to stand on a box in order to reach the microphone, but she leveled the room with the power and authority of her sincere humility and love for a hurting world. Heads of state and government dignitaries fought futilely to hold back their tears. God's love poured through her over the audience. She had elevated His deity above their dignity. The simplicity of her words was profound, the impact of her message, life changing.

Giving endlessly and fearlessly, without the slightest thought of what we'll get in return—that is love.

She often said, "The meaning of my life is the love of God. It is Christ in His distressing disguise whom I love and serve." She spoke often of the need for each one of us to pray to know the will of God for our lives, and for the grace to accept His way (as opposed to our own).

Mother Teresa's example of generosity and compassion toward the poor probably came from her own mother, who once told her, "When you do good, do it as if you were casting a stone into the depth of the sea." Mother Teresa listened to the voice of her mother and spent her life giving endlessly and fearlessly, without the slightest thought of what she might receive in return. That is love.

In 1979, when they gave Mother Teresa the prestigious Nobel Peace Prize, they said, "The loneliest, the most wretched, and the dying have at her hands received compassion without condescension, based on reverence for man." Mother Teresa,

in her own inimitable style, replied, "Personally, I am unworthy. I accept in the name of the poor."

We can learn a lot from this humble and powerful woman. She knew love intimately and did not hesitate to share it with all who were sent in her direction.

WHAT ABOUT MY PRINCE CHARMING?

Let me ask you first, are you fully prepared to be his Cinderella, First Lady, or Mrs. Right? Are you everything you expect that your Mr. Right, a.k.a. Prince Charming, would want? In other words, have you readied yourself? Have you taken inventory on your assets and liabilities? Have you taken your own "love quotient" lately? Let me put it this way: If you were him, would you pick you? Are you prepared to put this man's needs before your own if that is required? Are you ready to love him even if he snores, burps, forgets to bring you flowers, and tells the same stories over and over and over again?

Let's be clear on one thing. There is NO perfect person, male or female. This is one reason why there are so many divorces today. We are disappointed when the picture we've had of our perfect mate becomes smudged or wrinkled; then, instead of working with what we have left of our pristine, perfect Adonis, we throw him away and draw a new picture. Love is patient, love is kind, love *"bears all things, believes all things, hopes all things, endures all things. Love never fails"* (1 Corinthians 13:7–8).

FIRST, LOVE YOURSELF

That sounds very egocentric! It isn't. The truth is, until you really love yourself, you can't love anyone else. You can't

give away what you don't have. Until you fully accept the fact that you are worth loving, you will not be able to receive love from anyone else, much less give it. Our failure to love ourselves is the reason that we can't love other people the way God commanded us to.

The Bible tells us to *"love your neighbor as yourself"* (Galatians 5:14).

If people really knew God loved them, they would love Him back!

When I first read that, I realized why I'd been having so many problems with relationships...I didn't love myself. In fact, I didn't even really like myself! I was very hard on myself and had unrealistic expectations of how I should be. It was difficult for me to accept the fact that God really loved me because I had never known love before. God demonstrates His own love for us in this: *"While we were still sinners, Christ died for us"* (Romans 5:8)

The only way we can love God and love others is if we first know that we are loved. If you ask most people, "Do you know God loves you?" they will say, "Yes, of course." But they don't know God loves them because if they really knew God loved them, they would love Him back! And they would be able to love others. You can only love God when you know He will never leave you or forsake you. When you know that, you can then know His love and love Him in return.

So how do you learn to love yourself? You learn by realizing that God doesn't make junk! And that you were *"fearfully and wonderfully made"* (Psalm 139:14). Regardless of what anyone else may think (including you!), you are worthy of love because you are a child of God, and He is your true Father. He

created you in His very own image; and He loves you just the way you are...but He loves you too much to leave you that way.

I may not be all that I want to be, but thank God, I'm not what I used to be! God has done a huge work in me, and He will do the same for you. Let Him change your mind about who you really are.

We all have faults and weaknesses as a result of past experiences and wrong choices, but that doesn't mean we are worthless or unworthy to be loved. God wants us to believe and say, "I can love what God can love. I don't love everything I do, but I accept myself because God accepts me. I know I need to change. That is why I thank God for His promise that He *will perfect that which concerns me'* (Psalm 138:8). Meanwhile, I have His guarantee that when I mess up, if I go to Him and confess my mess, He will be faithful to forgive me and cleanse me from my wrong choices. (See 1 John 1:9.)"

God made you. God loves you.
God believes in you.

This confession, made daily, will help you renew your mind with the truth about who you are: God made me. God loves me. God values me. God believes in me. I am a member of God's family. I am part of God's plan. I am an instrument in God's kingdom and the apple of His eye!

God tells us to love our enemies. Have you ever considered that maybe your worst enemy is really you? When it comes to our mistakes or shortcomings, we are usually our own worst critics. We tend to compare ourselves at our worst to others at their best. So, just like we need to shower our enemies with love in order to overcome what they've done to us, we need to

shower ourselves with love to overcome what we've done to ourselves. If you can catch that revelation, it will change your life forever!

ABANDONED AND REJECTED

When a person has been abused, abandoned, or rejected in the past, the idea of totally trusting someone new can be terrifying. Many people actually reject themselves because somebody else rejected them. Anger, lack of self-confidence, jealousy, self-pity, and confusion begin to cloud the mind; and the person begins to build walls to protect himself from further pain. It hurts to be rejected. I experienced a lot of it as a child, as well as abandonment and abuse. I understand the pain. Because of it, I was determined that when I grew up, nobody would ever hurt me again...and the walls went up.

Nearly everyone experiences some kind of rejection at one time or another. Rejection can result from many causes: abandonment, abuse—including verbal, emotional, physical, and sexual—the death of a parent, unfaithfulness, divorce, or simply because a child was born the "wrong sex." My own father desperately wanted me to be a boy. Disappointed when I showed up as a girl, he said to my mother, "Well, since I can't give her my name, I'll give her my initials." He did, and I was stamped for life with the reminder that I "should have been a boy."

The word *rejection* means to be cast aside, to be thrown away as having no value. But the good news is that even though others may reject us, God never does. No matter how "bad" we've been, we can't do anything bad enough for God not to forgive and to make us brand-new again. His love is totally unconditional, and, as we accept it, He heals us from

all the rejection and abuse of our pasts. Total restoration is ours!

In raising my own son, I was very careful to distinguish the difference between what he did and who he was. He always knew that even though I sometimes did not like the things he did, I always loved him. And, although he sometimes did bad things, he was always good. He grew up a happy, confident, secure child, who was obedient and always knew that he was greatly loved. Many times throughout his childhood and young adulthood he would say to me, "Mom, I love my life! I can't imagine having a better life than I have. I am so lucky."

Even though others may reject us, God never does. His love is unconditional.

Needless to say, luck had nothing to do with it. When we make a decision to love, encourage, and empower others, it will lead them to a life of self-confidence and high self-esteem. In other words, they will feel loved and valued, just as God intended. On the other hand, we can also destroy a life, leaving it devoid of all goodness and joy, by speaking words of criticism, destruction, and death. The choice is ours.

A LOVE STORY

Elizabeth Barrett spent the first forty years of her life being tormented by her angry, controlling father. His constant rage made her sickly and she endured many illnesses that often kept her bedridden. But God, her true Father, had a plan for his precious daughter's escape. Enter a knight in shining armor, Robert Browning, who, after many a duel with Elizabeth's mean and brutal master, carried her off on his mighty

white stallion, where they traveled throughout Europe as their love for one another blossomed and grew. He didn't view her the way her earthly father had; instead, he saw her through the eyes of her heavenly Father, who loved her, treasured her, and wanted to protect and nurture her.

Robert loved her with all his being and encouraged her continually in her gift for writing. Most of us today are familiar with Elizabeth Barrett Browning's poetry, especially the sonnet "How Do I Love Thee?" which she wrote for her knight in shining armor.

See? Fairy tales do come true! So, yes, to finally answer your question, there *is* hope for true love for you.

Prayer for Love

Dear God,

Thank You for loving me. Help me to love like You do... unconditionally. Help me to see the good in others instead of the bad. Help me to forgive those who have hurt me in the past, knowing that You have forgiven me, even at my worst.

Show me myself through Your eyes, the eyes of love. Remind me that I'm a work in progress, being crafted perfectly by the Master Potter. Teach me to be kind and merciful to myself.

Help me to know Your love and to share it with others, to give more and take less. Make me right in Your sight and a light in a dark and dying world.

Mostly, dear God, help me to trust You always, and in all things, knowing that no matter what it looks like, feels like, or seems like, You are there by my side, taking me through, and leading me to my Promised Land. Amen.

Chapter Seven

DISCOURAGEMENT
What Am I Doing Wrong?

DISCOURAGEMENT
What Am I Doing Wrong?

Dear God,

Why can't I get all the way through to victory? I get very close, and then things collapse! I get almost out of debt, and then my car breaks down. I was recently offered the perfect job, and then suddenly, it was given to someone else. What am I doing wrong? I am weary and discouraged.

D iscouragement comes when we feel that our opportunity for success is gone forever, and we begin to see ourselves as less than we really are. If left alone for too long, discouragement can lead to depression.

Some signs of depression are: sadness, pessimism, hopelessness, worthlessness, helplessness, low or no energy, and lack of confidence in making decisions. Does this sound like a television commercial? These days, we can't watch TV for more than five or six minutes without seeing an advertisement for the latest antidepressant...guaranteed to "make you feel like yourself again!" The truth is, although antidepressants can cure chemical imbalances, they do not magically remove your problems. They only mask the symptoms. Depression will put you in a position to lose everything you have, but faith will put you in a position to receive everything God has for you.

Faith puts you in a position to receive everything God has for you.

When we feel depressed, we need to give ourselves a major attitude adjustment. One of the best ways to begin to see your situation in a more positive light is to do something to help those who are sick or down, such as a trip to the children's cancer ward. After spending a couple of hours with these precious children, your problems won't seem nearly as big. If you could see the hope and positive attitudes of these innocent babes, you would find the strength to face your own situation. When we feel down and discouraged, we need to stand up and fight.

You were predestined to live a successful and abundant life! What God has for you is for you! Nobody can take that away from you unless you voluntarily hand it over by giving up. Don't quit! Quitters never win, and winners never quit. Winston Churchill was a man well known for never giving up. The following quote epitomizes his refusal to entertain even the thought of failure:

We shall go on to the end, we shall fight in France, we shall fight on the seas and oceans, we shall fight with growing confidence and growing strength in the air, we shall defend our Island, whatever the cost may be, we shall fight on the beaches, we shall fight on the landing grounds, we shall fight in the fields and in the streets, we shall fight in the hills; we shall never surrender, and even if, which I do not for a moment believe, this Island or a large part of it were subjugated and starving, then our Empire beyond the seas, armed and guarded by the British Fleet, would carry on the struggle, until, in God's good time, the New World, with all its power and might, steps forth to the rescue and the liberation of the old. [1]

Wow! Just read that a few times and you'll be ready to run back out into battle!

We must fight depression at all costs because it leads to nothing.

THE JONESES

Often people give up and become discouraged due to lack of encouragement and support from their family and friends. We need to realize that not everybody is going to understand our vision, much less support it, because it's not for them. What God has for you is for you. Let the Joneses do whatever they need to do. Their life is not yours.

One of the hardest things God had to work out of me was my concern for the opinions of man. Because I had grown up with abandonment and rejection, I desperately wanted to excel and succeed in things in order to win love and approval. I can still hear my mother's voice ringing, "What will the neighbors

think?" I remember often wondering, "Why is she always so concerned about what the neighbors think when she doesn't care at all about what I think or feel?" And yet, true to the text-book, I followed in her footsteps and spent most of my adult life worrying about other people's opinions of me.

After much patience on God's part, and repeated failures on mine, God, in His wonderful gentleness, brought me to the realization that His opinion of me made man's opinion irrelevant. And the fact is, He loves me.

Sammy Davis Jr., whom I got to spend some time with during his brief role on *General Hospital*, shared some great wisdom with us one day. He said, "I don't know all the rules for success, but I know the sure way to fail: Try to please everyone." I often remind myself of his advice.

Then there is Charlie Brown. Remember Charlie Brown? Well one day Charlie Brown was talking with Lucy. He held out his hands to her and said, "Look at these hands! These hands may someday build big bridges! These hands might hit home runs! These hands could one day write important books, or heal sick people...or drive a rocket ship to Mars!" Lucy looked at Charlie Brown's hands and said, "They've got jelly on 'em." She didn't see what he saw. Not everyone is going to see what you see. Most people will just see the jelly. Be prepared to be misunderstood.

The sure way to fail is to try to please everyone.

As you accept the challenge to "go it alone," if need be, and to let go of negative people who constantly discourage you, God will supernaturally bring new people into your life who will support your vision and help you achieve your God-given

goal. They will be people who have already paid the price that you are now willing to pay. They will see the greatness in you and help you develop it. Remember, people are like elevators; they're either lifting you up or bringing you down.

THE ULTIMATE DISCOURAGEMENT

One day, King David and his mighty men returned from battle to find that their enemy had burned their city to the ground and taken their wives and children captive. The Bible says that King David and his men *"wept, until they had no more power to weep"* (1 Samuel 30:4). As if King David's grief wasn't great enough, when his men finally stopped weeping, they decided to stone him to death.

People are like elevators; they're either lifting you up or bringing you down.

I don't know what you're dealing with today, but very likely, it is not worse than the loss of everything and everyone you love, plus the betrayal of those you thought were on your side. Watch what King David did at one of the lowest points in his life: *"David strengthened* ["encouraged," KJV] *himself in the* LORD *his God"* (1 Samuel 30:6). In other words, David prayed. He didn't have a nervous breakdown, call his therapist, or pop a pill; he prayed. He reminded himself of all the times his mighty God had taken him through trials and into triumph in the past, and he asked God what he should do now. *"Shall I pursue this troop? Shall I overtake them?"* David asked. And God replied, *"Pursue, for you shall surely overtake them and without fail recover all"* (verse 8).

David listened to God, believed God, and then acted on the instructions God had given him. He took four hundred

of his men, went after his enemies, and *"David recovered all"* (verse 18)—all that the enemy had stolen from him, including his two wives, sons, and daughters. Prayer works! And God is faithful!

DISCOURAGEMENT DISSECTED

William A. Ward describes discouragement in its entirety. He says,

Discouragement is dissatisfaction with the past, distaste for the present, and distrust of the future. It is ingratitude for the blessings of yesterday, indifference to the opportunities of today, and insecurity regarding strength for tomorrow. It is unawareness of the presence of beauty, unconcern for the needs of our fellow man, and unbelief in the promises of old. It is impatience with time, immaturity of thought, and impoliteness to God. [2]

Let's break it down:

MAN HAS	GOD SAYS
Dissatisfaction with the past	*"Forgetting those things which are behind and reaching forward to those things which are ahead"* (Philippians 3:13).
Distaste for the present	*"Giving thanks always for all things to God"* (Ephesians 5:20).
Distrust of the future	*"Trust in the LORD with all your heart, and lean not on your own understanding"* (Proverbs 3:5).

81

MAN HAS	GOD SAYS
Ingratitude for the blessings of yesterday	*"Forget not all His benefits"* (Psalm 103:2).
Indifference to the opportunities of today	*"This is the day the LORD has made; we will rejoice and be glad in it"* (Psalm 118:24).
Insecurity regarding strength for tomorrow	*"Do not worry about tomorrow, for tomorrow will worry about its own things"* (Matthew 6:34).
Unawareness of the presence of beauty	*"When I consider Your heavens, the work of Your fingers, the moon and the stars, which You have ordained"* (Psalm 8:3).
Unconcern for the needs of our fellow men	*"He who has mercy on the poor, happy is he"* (Proverbs 14:21).
Unbelief in the promises of old	*"He who promised is faithful"* (Hebrews 10:23).
Impatience with time	*"To everything there is a season, a time for every purpose under heaven"* (Ecclesiastes 3:1).
Immaturity of thought	*"When I was a child, I spoke as a child...but when I became a man, I put away childish things"* (1 Corinthians 13:11).
Impoliteness to God	*"Where were you when I laid the foundations of the earth?"* (Job 38:4).

THE FINAL WORD

If God commanded us to take *"dominion over...all things"* (Psalm 8:6), and He meant it (see Genesis 1:26–29); and if He gave us authority and power through Christ *"over all the power of the enemy,"* and He did according to Luke 10:19; then why are so many people struggling to pay their bills, to succeed in their businesses, and to stay out of divorce court?

I believe that part of the answer is given to us in Daniel 7:25, where God warned us that in the end times, which many believe we are living in right now, our enemy, Satan, *"shall persecute the saints of the Most High."* The literal translation for *persecute* is "to wear out."

As we rest in God, we become restored, renewed, and revitalized.

Many people today are simply worn-out. Why? They haven't learned to rest in God. They've forgotten that the battle is the Lord's and that God exhorts us in Hebrews 4:9–11 that we must labor "to enter His rest." And God says that when we work for Him, His *"yoke is easy"* and His *"burden is light"* (Matthew 11:30).

As we rest in God, we become restored, renewed, and revitalized. Once we are at rest, and no longer stressed, He can then begin to strengthen us, give us His game plan, and empower us to return again to the battlefield. Only this time, we will reign victorious. Now it's impossible to rest in God if you don't really believe that He will come through for you, and the only way to possess that certainty is through intimacy with Him. When you get to know Him, you will begin to trust Him. When you trust Him, He will fight for you. When He fights for you, you will win! *"Commit your way to the LORD, trust also in Him, and He shall bring it to pass"* (Psalm 37:5).

Prayer of Encouragement

Dear God,

Thank You for reminding me that You've got it all under control. Help me to trust You more in the future than I have in the past. Help me to remember the price You paid, not only for my freedom but also for my victory and authority on this earth.

Help me to stop comparing myself with others by remembering that You made me exactly the way You wanted me to be, no mistakes. Please forgive me for allowing myself to become discouraged by my circumstances, and help me to always remember those things You've done for me in the past. You are so faithful.

Please lead me in the way I should go. Open those doors that You want me to walk through, and close every door that does not lead to Your will for my life. Help me to remain positive in a negative world and to encourage myself when others don't.

Thank You for Your patience. Thank You for Your love. Amen.

---

[1] Churchill, Winston. "We Shall Fight on the Beaches." June 4, 1940. <http://www.quoteland.com/library/speeches/churchill1.asp> (29 July 2004)

[2] <http://www.preparingforeternity.org/history/Ward/william_ward.htm> (29 July 2004)

Chapter Eight

ANGER

Take It Away!

Chapter Eight

ANGER
Take It Away!

Dear God,

Why do I snap so often? I've been trying for years to get my anger under control, and it's not getting any better. The worst part is that the people I'm hurting the most are those closest to me. They don't deserve it. I'm at the end of my rope. Please help me.

First of all, know that you are not alone. Many people struggle with anger and rage. I'm not saying that it's okay to allow anger and rage to reign and rule in your life, but sometimes it's comforting to know that not only are you not alone but there is also hope and help available.

In this Columbine, 9-11, Afghanistan/Iraq conflict world we're living in, it's no wonder people are angry. Where do we turn? Who can we trust? What should we do? America is not Mayberry anymore. (Was it ever?)

Road rage is on the rise. A few short years ago we wouldn't have understood what that term meant. Now we drive in fear of it.

Recently on network news it was announced that murder is now the second leading cause of death in teenagers. What are we doing? What are we not doing? Why are the ones we love the most, our children, having to live in a world filled with such violence and fear?

God tells us to *"cease from anger, and forsake wrath"* (Psalm 37:8) and to *"make no friendship with an angry man"* (Proverbs 22:24). He also says that *"he who is slow to anger is better than the mighty"* (Proverbs 16:32). Hmmm, perhaps we just need to get back to Bible basics. What a concept!

SMALL BEGINNINGS

Anger comes from pain. Often, it comes from pain that was inflicted knowingly or unknowingly during a person's early childhood. Because a small child doesn't know how to process, much less understand, mistreatment from adults who are supposed to love her, she often buries that pain deep down inside.

The problem arises when that child grows up and "buttons" are pushed that emotionally remind that former child of things that happened to her years ago. The picture of the injustice is often erased from the conscious mind, but the subconscious "feeling" part of the brain has not lost the image. So the smallest, seemingly unrelated incident can trigger an

87

outrageous response in this former victim. This response is so far out of balance that the person it is directed at is often confused and terrified, especially if it is a small child. It's as if someone you loved told you out of simple concern that you had spinach in your teeth, and you pulled out a gun and shot him...overkill!

We must identify where our anger comes from. Anger comes from pain.

I personally struggled with anger and rage for many years until God began to show me its origin. Because of my childhood, I had buried a lot of hurt and pain, but eventually it came up and out, surprising everyone, including me. I didn't understand why I could go from zero to ninety in one second flat, emotionally speaking. It was like a volcano inside of me over which I felt I had absolutely no control. I lived daily dreading the next eruption, which would always come out of left field and appear to be totally unrelated to whatever situation I was in at that moment. I hated myself. And I hated even more that my anger was usually directed at the ones I loved the most.

GIVE ME SOME HOPE!

I was desperate. I began to pray and ask God to take the anger away. In His wisdom, He didn't. Instead, He began to reveal to me, slowly and gently, where the anger had come from. He began to unveil to me, in direct proportion to what I could handle, the injustices I had endured as a small child and how I had swallowed and buried those painful things in an effort to make them disappear. Little did I know then that, decades later, these "secrets" would have to be dealt with.

I'd like to be able to tell you that it was a quick and effortless process, but that would be a lie. The good news is that God, in all His awesome love and mercy, did change me over time. He convinced me, through His Word, that if I truly put my trust in Him, He could and would heal me. And as I did choose to trust in Him and confessed His Word over my situation, I began to see the anger disappear. At first I remember noticing that it had been over a week since I'd been upset, then several weeks, then a month, then several months. Today I honestly could not tell you when the last "episode" of anger took place. It's been many, many years. He was true to His word: *"He who has begun a good work in you will complete it"* (Philippians 1:6).

WHAT CAN I DO?

First of all, you can't do it alone. You know that's true because you've already tried. How many times? You're going to need God's help. Be comforted, He wants you free from this anger even more than you want to be free, and He is well able to get the job done. All you have to do is trust Him and cooperate.

When you hook up with God, His power, and His Word, nothing can defeat you.

I want to share with you one of the Scriptures that proved most effective in my own dealing with the spirit of anger that had such a hold on me. Psalm 18:37 says, *"I have pursued my enemies and overtaken them; neither did I turn back again till they were destroyed."* Sometimes you simply have to get mad. You have to go to war against that thing, just as you would go to war against someone who was trying to break into your house and steal everything that belongs to you. The Bible tells

us that *"the kingdom of heaven suffers violence, and the violent take it by force"* (Matthew 11:12)

I got violent! I was determined to get rid of the anger and rage that was destroying my life, my joy, my peace. I refused to be refused and denied to be denied. God said it. I believed it. That settled it. I would win. That was that. When you adopt this mind-set and hook up with God, His power, and His Word, there is nothing that can defeat you. You, too, can be freed from inappropriate and uncontrollable anger. That is a promise—not from me but from God, who says that He is *"no respecter of persons"* (Acts 10:34 KJV). What he did for me, He will do for you.

AN ANGRY MAN

Most of us know the story about Cain and Abel. Cain and Abel were the sons of Adam and Eve. One day the two young men brought offerings to God. God accepted the offering that Abel brought, but He rejected the offering from Cain. (See Genesis 4:1–8.)

Cain was hurt, jealous, and angry at his brother—so angry, in fact, that he killed him.

God spoke with Cain before he had committed this horrible act of violence and asked him why he was so angry. God also told Cain *"you should rule over* [the anger]" (Genesis 4:7). Cain did not, and the first murder was committed. When we don't know how to keep our emotions under control but instead allow our feelings and emotions to rule over us, we become slaves to those emotions.

Notice that God told Cain he should *rule over* the anger. God never tells us to do something we are not able to do. Therefore, it would have been possible for Cain to get a grip on his feelings and not kill his brother. The interesting thing is

that Abel had done nothing at all to his brother. Cain's anger stemmed strictly from the rejection he had received from God. But instead of owning the fact that he had presented an unacceptable offering, and perhaps going ahead and making things right between himself and God, Cain chose to put the blame on Abel. God had even tried to reason with Cain earlier, saying, *"If you do well, will you not be accepted?"* (Genesis 4:7). Cain knew he had not done right in God's sight, yet instead of stepping up to the plate, humbling himself, and making things right, he kept his ego intact and made a decision to put the blame elsewhere. Looking in the mirror is not always easy.

God never tells us to do something we are not able to do.

Sometimes, when we get angry, we do the same thing. We blame somebody else for our anger because it's easier than taking the responsibility for it. It's easier to shift the blame onto an innocent party rather than to deal with the demons inside of us that keep dragging us down and justifying their right to exist. Remember, that which you tolerate, you will keep.

Here's the good news: You can be free! Whether you choose to or not is totally up to you. You can remain bound to that darkness that haunts your life, or you can make a decision that you're going to do whatever it takes to be set free. The choice is yours and yours alone. Nobody else can make it for you.

SHOW ME MORE

God says, *"Let not your heart be troubled"* (John 14:1). Therefore, you have control over whether or not your heart will be troubled. Proverbs 4:23 NIV tells us to *"guard your heart."* You are not always in control of your circumstances, but you are

always in control of your heart. How do you guard your heart? You guard your heart by not allowing negative things from the outside to get inside. In other words, when trouble comes (and it will come), you make a choice to not let it bother you. How do you do that? You do that by refusing to accept the trouble and trusting in God instead.

My God will supply all my needs according to His riches.

Here is an example: Your bank calls you to let you know that, because you can't pay your mortgage, they are going to repossess your house. Instead of getting all upset, crying and feeling sorry for yourself, you grab hold of what God says about your situation. You begin to speak boldly, "No! The bank will NOT repossess my home. *My God will supply all my needs according to His riches. No good thing will He withhold from me,* and this house is a good thing. I don't care what this situation looks like, sounds like, seems like, or feels like. I don't walk by what I see or feel. I walk by the Word of God, which promises me that He will fight my battles, and if He says He will, then He will, because God can't lie. *"With God, all things are possible"* (Matthew 19:26), and *"all"* includes keeping my house! Thank you Lord, for the victory!" (See Philippians 4:19 and Psalm 84:11.)

OK, I'M READY. WHERE DO I START?
THREE STEPS TO FREEDOM:

1. Give it to God. (And don't take it back!) *"Casting all your care upon Him, for He cares for you"* (1 Peter 5:7). Realize and accept that you cannot do this alone and that He has been waiting for you to come to Him for help. Until you realize you can't, He won't.

2. Keep your mind and your eyes on Him. *"You will keep him in perfect peace, whose mind is stayed on You"* (Isaiah 26:3). When anger starts to grab you by the throat, close your mouth, back away from the situation, take a deep breath, and look to God. At first you may have to do this several times a day; but the more you do it, the easier it becomes. Don't be discouraged if you sometimes fail. You will. Just pick yourself up, brush yourself off, get back in the ring, and remember God loves you! You are a work in progress.

3. Remain confident that He will finish it. *"He who has begun a good work in you will complete it"* (Philippians 1:6). The only way you will lose this battle is if you decide to give up. Don't. Choose to go the distance (however long it takes), and you will surely win. God can't lie. God is truth. When He says He will do something, He always does it. That, my friend, you can take to the bank.

Prayer for Freedom

Dear God,

I want to be free from anger, rage, and pain. Please help me to cast all my cares on You and to trust You to help me. Deliver me from the sins of my past and from the sins of my parents. Help me to forgive those who have hurt me in the past and erase the memories that trigger my angry outbursts.

Please forgive me for all the pain I have caused others, and heal them from any related damage. Ask them to forgive me, too; and help me to forgive myself. I trust You, God, to change me. Give me the courage and the patience to win this victory. I know that with You, God, nothing is impossible. Thank You. Amen.

Chapter Nine

FEAR

Your Greatest Enemy

Chapter Nine

FEAR

Your Greatest Enemy

Dear God,

Why am I always afraid of things? I start out with a positive attitude, but before I realize it, I'm caught in an overwhelming fear of failure. It's as though I'm defeated before I ever begin.

I really want to break this cycle. I am starting a new job soon, and if I can't make this one work, I'm afraid I will not only lose the love and respect of my family, but I will lose everything I have. Please help me.

According to Webster's dictionary, *fear* is alarm and agitation caused by the expectation or realization of danger. Notice that fear can be experienced either through something that actually takes place or by simple expectation that something might take place.

Think about how many times you worried yourself crazy over something that never came to pass. Worry is fear. Fear and faith cannot coexist; they are flip sides of the same coin. The Bible tells us, *"Do not fret; it only causes harm"* (Psalm 37:8). When I first discovered that information, I became terrified! "Oh no," I said, "I've already got enough trouble! I don't want to cause any more by 'fretting'! But, how do I not fret?"

Although we don't always have control over our circumstances, we do have control over how we deal with those circumstances.

Although we don't always have control over our circumstances, we do always have control over how we are going to deal with those circumstances. We can be fearful, (full of fear) or we can be faithful (full of faith). *"Faith is the substance of things hoped for, the evidence of things not seen"* (Hebrews 11:1). In other words, you cannot see it with your human eyes, but you can see it through the eyes of your imagination.

Studies have proven that your life moves in the direction of your most dominant thoughts. If you are constantly thinking about those things you do not want to happen, or living in fear of what might happen, then those fearful things are what you will draw into your life. Your mind is like a magnet. Whatever you focus on, you will attract. That is why God tells us to meditate on good things. *"Whatever things are true, whatever things are noble, whatever things are just, whatever things are*

pure, whatever things are lovely, whatever things are of good report, if there is any virtue and if there is anything praiseworthy; meditate on these things" (Philippians 4:8). When we do, these things will find their way into our lives.

Here's a good example: One of my sisters grew up fearing that one day she would get married and have a severely handicapped child. She began to think these thoughts as a young teenager. The more she would dwell on these negative images in her mind, the more fearful she became of the possibility that those "pictures" would become her reality. Now there was no basis for her fear. She had been born perfectly healthy, and there was no genetic defect waiting to be passed down through her to her children.

It's time to believe God for the absolute best...because that's what He desires for us.

Many years later, however, my sister married and had a son. During the birth of the child, his oxygen levels were not being properly monitored, and as a result of the oxygen deprivation, he developed cerebral palsy. Her life had moved in the direction of her most dominant thoughts.

If we were to be honest and take a look at our lives, we would see that, although we didn't always get everything we wanted, we did get pretty much what we expected. It's time to lift our expectations! Raise the bar! Or "kick it up a notch!" as Emeril would say. It's time to believe God for the absolute best...because that is what He desires for us.

CHALLENGE YOUR FEAR!

Julius II, a patron of the arts, asked Michelangelo to paint a design on the ceiling and walls of the Sistine Chapel in the

Vatican. Michelangelo declined due to fear of the fact that he had never before attempted a work of that magnitude.

Julius refused to be refused and would not allow Michelangelo to deny his request. He had already seen the genius in this unique and powerful artist.

Fearful and trapped, Michelangelo, having no choice, began the overwhelming task. To this day, Michelangelo's creation in the Sistine Chapel remains one of the most awesome, inspiring, and powerful paintings a man has ever produced.

Surround yourself with positive people who are always expecting the best in life.

Sometimes you need to simply jump in, face your fear, and as Nike would say, "Just Do It!" If you try and fail, at least you've tried. If you don't ever try, you won't ever know. Often others can see potential in you that you cannot. That is one reason why it is important to surround yourself with positive people who are always striving for and expecting the best in life, as opposed to negative drainers who seem to find every excuse to defend their (and your) limitations.

Someone once said that fear was False Evidence Appearing Real. When you stop and think about it, that's exactly what it is. When I was a child, I had a constant recurring nightmare. I was afraid to go to bed because I knew that the minute I went to sleep I would experience the same horrible thing again. I dreamed that my teddy bear, which I loved and took with me everywhere, turned into the devil and tried to strangle me to death...false evidence appearing real.

As children, we often cannot separate the real from the unreal. But, as adults, we have the necessary components to

decipher which is the true item. Therefore, we have the ability to take authority over those false images and replace them with whatever pictures we desire.

In chapter two, *Faith,* we talked about how to step out of the boat and create a successful life. Abraham Lincoln gave us a perfect example of how to rise above the fear of failure by faith and create the world we desire. When we do this, we are not talking about doing something hocus pocus or New Age, rather, we are imitating our heavenly Father who *"calls those things which do not exist as though they did"* (Romans 4:17). That is faith. What does this have to do with fear? I'm so glad you asked!

FIGHT TO THE DEATH!

We are talking about how to conquer fear. Your fear is not going to disappear miraculously one day. In order to get rid of it, you must take authority over it. But, before you can take authority over it, you have to first identify it. Get specific. Where did it come from? What does it feel like? When does it appear? Does it ever go away? When was the last time you can remember not having this fear in your life?

When you begin to ask yourself these specific questions, you begin to expose this spirit. You narrow down the suspects, like in a police lineup when they're looking for the bad guy. Make no mistake; this spirit of fear is your enemy. You need to track it down, confront it, and then destroy it. Left alone, it will steal every good thing you have—from your joy, to your health, to your bank account. Remember, *"God has not given us a spirit of fear, but of power and of love and of a sound mind"* (2 Timothy 1:7).

Franklin D. Roosevelt stated it beautifully in his first inaugural address on May 4, 1933: "The only thing we have to fear is fear itself." Fear will paralyze you if you let it.

Over and over again in His Word, God tells us not to be afraid, to "fear not" and instead to "be bold and very courageous" (Deuteronomy 31:8; Isaiah 44:8; Joshua 10:25). He explained in Isaiah 43:5 why we don't have to be afraid: *"For I am with you."*

But how do I know that God is with me, you ask? If you really don't know, you can know without any doubt that He is there with you. He says, *"You do not have because you do not ask"* (James 4:2). Have you asked Him to come into your life? Our Lord is a gentleman. He will not force His way into anyone's life. *"I stand at the door and knock. If anyone hears My voice and opens the door, I will come in to him and dine with him, and he with Me"* (Revelation 3:20).

In His Word, God tells us, "Fear not, but be bold and courageous."

God gave you free will. You get to choose. You can continue to deal with things as you have in the past, or you can invite Him in and let Him deal with them while you watch in awe as He does. I highly recommend the second choice.

FEAR FACTOR

Fear is so prevalent in our world today that it has even been given its own television series. We human beings seem to have a sick affinity for fear. *The Exorcist*, in all of its gore, drew millions to the box office. It was reported that the day the movie premiered from coast to coast, many were leaving the theaters violently ill. Others were plagued with a spirit of fear for months and even years after viewing the show. My former pastor, Rod Parsley, was one of them. He shared with us one day how he and a few of his Bible school buddies

decided it would be fun to go see the movie. For nearly two years afterward, he was afraid even to leave his own home.

Several years ago, in 1990, I spoke with the director of *The Exorcist*, who informed me that after the filming of the movie, many members of the cast and crew had been hospitalized with sudden serious illnesses, while others died mysterious deaths. The lead actress, Linda Blair, wound up in a mental hospital. He also said that members of this same group, ranging from grips to actors and even to him—a former Academy Award winner—had not been able to get another job since. The devil will use you, abuse you, and then throw you away. The spirit of fear is real. Don't invite it in.

In 1962 we took prayer out of our schools. The very next year President John F. Kennedy was shot. It was a simple prayer, something like, "Dear God, please bless us, our families, our friends, our country, and our president. Amen," but it created a spiritual covering of protection in the heavenlies. We shot a hole in that covering when we removed that corporate prayer, uttered daily out of the mouths of innocent, loving children. Through that hole, fear found a place to enter America. Before long, Columbine, 9-11, and terrorist camps right here in the United States became our new reality.

Prayer works. Surely there had been hundreds, if not thousands, of terrorist threats to our country throughout previous years, but those threats remained idle threats until we gave them an entrance by blasting a hole in our prayer covering. That hole continues to grow bigger each day as many now fight to remove "In God We Trust" from our money, take "one nation under God" from the Pledge of Allegiance, and incorporate same-sex marriages into our society.

But here's some good news. Here is an awesome example of God's love for us in spite of our bad selves: *"If My people who are called by My name will humble themselves, and pray and seek My face, and turn from their wicked ways, then I will hear from heaven, and will forgive their sin and heal their land"* (2 Chronicles 7:14). Notice that He's not talking about atheists or others who don't believe in Him. He says *"if My people."* We need to pray. And when we do, God's grace is so big that, no matter how badly we have failed, He is always there to help us get back up again.

No matter how badly we have failed, God is always there to help us get back up again.

Whether it's freedom from personal fear, fear for your country, or fear of the future, your prayers are the answer. *"Perfect love casts out fear"* (1 John 4:18). God is love. A more perfect love, you will not find.

Prayer for Deliverance

Dear God,

Please deliver me from fear. I cannot do it on my own. I am tired of living with inferiority, intimidation, and insecurity. I want to be bold and courageous as You have told me to be. I want to be the head and not the tail...above and not beneath. I want to be victorious in my life instead of a failure.

Help me to see myself as more than a conqueror! Let me look through Your eyes and view the potential You have placed inside of me, and then, Lord, help me to run with that vision into victory. And, God, I pray, please heal our land. Amen.

Chapter Ten

PEACE

Follow It!

Chapter Ten

PEACE
Follow It!

Dear God,

Help! There is so much chaos and confusion in my life! I remember when I was a little girl, how I would lay in the grass and look up at the clouds, watching the images change as the gentle breeze turned a kitten into a dinosaur, or a lollipop into a palm tree. What I would give for even five minutes of that now!

How can I begin to create a more peaceful existence? I keep saying that I'm going to, but it seems like the harder I try, the busier I get! How can I enjoy life without letting it pass me by?

Peace

Peace: the elusive butterfly of the twenty-first century. Peace is what everyone wants, but few appropriate. Peace appears to fly right in the face of progress and elude the seeker at every turn—perhaps because chasing after peace is counterproductive to that which you are seeking.

Peace is more powerful than war and far more difficult to find. True peace, *"which surpasses all understanding"* (Philippians 4:7), can only be found in God. You cannot buy peace, sell peace, or order it online. Peace is free, but it will cost you the chaos in your life. It will require discipline in your daily walk and adjustments in your day planner.

True peace can only be found in God.

We have moved beyond the microwave generation into the supersonic spaceship age. Our computers advance as quickly as our clocks tick. Actually, it's been a long time since our clocks have ticked—now they're digital. We're able to fly to space and clone sheep. What's left? Where do we go from here? Those very thoughts are enough to prevent you from knowing peace. So what can you do?

You can begin at the beginning, which is right now. Yesterday's peace is history, and tomorrow never comes, so today—actually, this very moment—is all you can really count on. Start right where you are, erase the board, and draw a new picture of your life. Your mind is the drawing board of tomorrow's circumstances. If you really want peace in your life, you're going to have to make it a priority and create some new blueprints.

Personally, I am addicted to peace. I can't imagine life without it. Yet I used to live in chaos and uncertainty, with doubt and fear all around me. I made a decision years ago that peace

would be my number one objective and that I would find it, keep it, and dwell in it forever. It required a lot of adjustments in my life and the emptying out of old baggage. Mind-sets had to be replaced, and habits changed. Temptations promising excitement and danger had to be dealt with—brutally.

Peace means: the absence of war or other hostilities; freedom from quarrels or disagreement; inner contentment, serenity. While the world in general could use the first definition, most of us as individuals are seeking serenity and inner contentment. It is possible, and it is available.

Show Me the Way

While many today may suggest alternatives, I still hold fast to the fact that the only way to find true and lasting peace is through and in God. I can say this with some authority because I have tried most of the "alternatives" in the past. They didn't work. Some of them produced a false sense of peace for a moment or two, but confusion and chaos always returned.

One of the ways the world offers you peace is through transcendental meditation, or TM. I practiced it for many years; and, although it did force me to be still for twenty minutes twice a day, the other twenty-three hours and twenty minutes remained unchanged. Biofeedback was another popular tool years ago. It seemed like it might work so I gave it a try...again, nothing changed. Eventually I decided that perhaps if I just knew what was going to happen in my future, I would have more peace about my present, so I began to visit psychics, channelers, and fortune-tellers. Every now and then they would predict something that did eventually take place; but ninety percent of the time it was a total waste of my money,

my time, and, ironically, my peace of mind. I wound up right back where I had started...searching for peace.

You may not be involved in any of the things I just mentioned. For you, the search for peace may come in the form of a tuning out in front of the TV, sleeping when you feel stressed, or drowning your sorrows in drugs or alcohol. If that's you, you're simply choosing another form of a band-aid. It will come off eventually, and the wound underneath it will again be exposed. A temporary fix is the best you will get.

SHOW ME THE RIGHT WAY!

Don't you hate it when you ask someone for directions and they send you the wrong way? They tell you to go north when they mean south, or they say "turn left on Cherry Street," when you need to turn *right* on Cherry Street! Or, they take a wild guess (not wanting to appear stupid) and send you off on the wrong freeway! I hate that! It's a waste of your time, energy, and, once again, your peace of mind. People who do not know the right directions should not be allowed to give them! (When I am elected president, that will be the first rule I enforce.)

You must be willing to let go of everything in your life that is preventing your peace.

It's the same thing when you ask the world how to find peace—if you follow their road map, you'll just be traveling in circles.

Let's talk about the right way to find peace. First, you have to desire peace. Second, you have to be determined at all costs to acquire peace. Third, you must be willing to let go of

anything and everything in your life that is preventing your peace.

A spiritual spring-cleaning must be set into motion. Peace will not magically appear on your doorstep one fine day.

Practically speaking, make a list of all the things in your life that are now requiring your attention. Next, create categories to help you break that initial list down and put it into smaller groups. Your categories, for example, could be: family, business, health, friends, finances. And don't forget a special category for yourself! You need private time each day to keep your priorities straight and to connect with God. *"For God is not the author of confusion but of peace"* (1 Corinthians 14:33). And He promises that He *"will keep him in perfect peace, whose mind is stayed on You"* (Isaiah 26:3).

Order in your life is essential to peace.

One of the most common reasons many people never find peace in their lives is because of all the confusion they allow to exist around them. Order in your life is essential for peace. God is a God of order—just look at nature. So lose the clutter! Get rid of all the dead wood and excess. That includes not only the dirty dishes in your sink and the piles all over your house but those negative people in your life who are constantly creating chaos. Now if you have rebellious children, or a demanding husband, this doesn't include them. They are a result of the choices you have made, and they are your responsibility. Don't worry. God will help you! He promises you this: *"My grace is sufficient"* (2 Corinthians 12:9).

Back to the drawing board! All right, if you're still reading, that means that you have chosen to pursue peace. Good

choice! Now, if you haven't already, pick up an eraser in your mind and erase your past. Once you have done that, find a piece of paper and a pencil, pen, or crayon, and begin to draw a new picture of what you want your life to look like. How is it different from the old picture that you erased? What have you removed? What have you added? God tells us clearly to *"write the vision and make it plain"* (Habakkuk 2:2). If you don't have a clear picture of where you want to go, you will probably never arrive. It's like trying to take a trip without a map.

HIS PLAN OR YOURS?

If you have spent most of your life trying to live it your way, like I did, you might want to check out God's plan for you. He tells us clearly that He has a specific plan for each one of us. *"I know the thoughts that I think toward you, says the LORD, thoughts of peace and not of evil, to give you a future and a hope"* (Jeremiah 29:11).

God has a specific plan for each one of us.

In order to find out what God's plan for you is, you will need to do three things: stop, look, and listen. You must first stop the constant clamor around you! Turn off your cell phone, unplug your TV, put a "do not disturb" sign on your door, and wait on the Lord to speak. God speaks in a still, small voice that cannot be heard in the midst of chaos. Second, you must look honestly at your life and see those things that have to go. He will show you. Third, you have to be willing to listen as God guides you and follow as He leads you into His perfect plan. The desires of your heart will help you plan your way, but God will direct your steps. (See Psalm 16.)

After a very short while, these three steps will become a desire, and then a habit, which will turn into a lifestyle, giving you the peace you have been longing for. You will find that those things you used to spend so much time on were mere distractions, preventing you from living a loving, joyful, and peaceful life.

"KEEP MY PEACE IN YOUR HEART"

Several years ago during the Christmas holidays, I was spending some quiet time with God. As I looked at the beautiful tree with all the glistening lights and decorations, I began to thank Him for all His many blessings. It suddenly occurred to me to ask Him something I had never asked Him before. "Lord, instead of making another New Year's resolution like I normally do, what can I do for You this year? What would make You happy?" Without missing a beat He replied, "Keep My peace in your heart." Wow, I thought, what a nice thing to say. He hadn't even asked anything for Himself, just for me. "Okay, Lord, I will do it," I answered.

Little did I know that the upcoming year would prove to be the most difficult "peace-keeping" year of my entire life. The first six months were fairly easy. Peace reigned and flowed through my days. Whenever I did feel unrest begin to rise up, it was easy to simply shift my focus back to His peace and stay in the flow. Life was good.

Months seven, eight, and nine proved to be far more difficult. I was faced with emotional and relational issues of great magnitude, and keeping His peace in my heart was proving to be beyond challenging—bordering on impossible. I allowed myself to be swayed by others opinions, and I began to second-guess myself as my emotions clouded my vow. Before I knew

it, my peace had disappeared! Anxiety, confusion, and fear had replaced it. How could I have let this happen? I was devastated!

Desperate, I decided to go on a three-day fast and find the answer. It was then that God, in His awesome mercy and grace, showed me where I had gotten off track. I immediately repented and asked Him to do whatever it took to get me back where I belonged. He did. My peace returned, and, by His grace, I will never lose it again.

God is there to pick you up, brush you off, and get you back where you belong.

Why did I tell you this story? I shared this most intimate chapter of my life with you so that, if you ever get off track and lose your peace like I did, you will have reassurance that, since *"God is no respecter of persons"* (Acts 10:34 KJV), He will also be there to pick you up, brush you off, and help get you back where you belong. He is so faithful!

Pursue peace! It is the one thing that will keep love in your life, hope in your heart, and a smile on your face.

Prayer for Peace

Dear God,

Please help me to find peace. Show me how to replace the distractions and chaos of my life with order. Teach me to listen, as You lead me, and to be obedient to follow as You direct my steps. Remind me daily to stay connected to You, the Prince of Peace, because You love me even more that I love myself.

Take me back to those early days of watching the clouds go by. Help me to remember that total surrender, knowing that You have everything under control.

God, I pray also for the peace of our country. Please continue to bless us and to remind us to pray for our leaders, our soldiers, and our government. Forgive us for wandering from Your ways. Bring us back to the foundation upon which You built these United States, one nation, under God. Amen.

Chapter Eleven

ENVY

Why Not Me?

Chapter Eleven

ENVY
Why Not Me?

Dear God,

Why am I always so envious of others? I hate feeling that way, but I just can't help it. I feel like I get the last pick of everything. I know that it's wrong to be jealous, but I don't know how to stop feeling that way. Sometimes I even get angry when my friends tell me about good things that have happened to them. What's wrong with me? How can I change this bad attitude?

This will be a short chapter because, frankly, there are not many good things to say about envy except that it has to go!

You have been created in the image of God. Why do you want to change the plan He has for you? Are you looking for something better than what He knows you need?

Usually a low self-image is at the core of envy. Have you taken a good long look in the mirror lately? What do you see? Do you only see the negative things? Or do you look at the good things about yourself and your life? What you look for is what you will find.

First of all, it's important to realize that we often compare ourselves at our worst to others at their best. Your neighbor, who looks so classy as she leaves for work in her Armani suit, driving her new Mercedes, may have problems that she hides from the world. Maybe she cries herself to sleep every night because her marriage is on the rocks. And quite possibly, she has the same envious thoughts about you as she watches you play with your kids in the backyard.

We often compare ourselves at our worst to others at their best.

That man you wish your husband would emulate may be abusive to his wife and children who have been hiding that side of him from you.

That big home you've been longing for may have put the past four tenants into bankruptcy due to problems you aren't aware of.

My point is this: Don't judge anyone or anything by what you can see with your eyes because you're probably not viewing the whole picture. God tells us clearly in His Word that those who *"measure themselves"* or *"compare themselves"* with others are *"not wise"* (2 Corinthians 10:12 NIV).

117

LET'S GET WISE

First of all, I want you to take an inventory of all the good things about yourself. Start with whatever comes into your mind. Are you kind? Are you generous? A good listener? Are you compassionate to those less fortunate?

Let's look at the physical side. What is there about yourself that you do like? Have you been blessed with pretty hair, nice teeth, or beautiful eyes? How about your skin, your smile, or your hands? Surely there is something you can point to that you are glad to have. Start with that thing, and begin to thank God for it.

The quickest way out of envy is to identify the things that God has blessed you with.

Next, begin to look around your life and notice other things that God has blessed you with. Maybe He's given you wonderful parents or a great child or friend. Maybe you have a job or a talent that others would love to have. I guarantee that, as you begin to look for the good things in your life, you will find them. God doesn't leave anybody out. He loves us all.

The quickest way to exit the room of self-pity and envy is through the door of thanksgiving. As you begin to be grateful for what you already have, then and only then will God begin to bless you with more. He longs to give you the desires of your heart, but first He must be able to trust you with what He has already given you.

Remember the tenth commandment? *"You shall not covet your neighbor's house; you shall not covet your neighbor's wife, nor his male servant, nor his female servant, nor his ox, nor his donkey,*

nor anything that is your neighbor's" (Exodus 20:17). When we are jealous of anything that belongs to someone else, we are in direct disobedience to God. It's like a slap in the face to Him. We are saying, in effect, that He did a bad job, that He messed up, that He forgot something.

He is God. He is perfect. If anyone has messed up, it's us!

GUILTY AS CHARGED

Several months ago, God told me that I had been coveting. I was shocked when He said it! "Me?" I asked. He simply nodded yes. (Have you ever noticed that God never answers stupid questions?) "How, Lord?" I asked again, "I am not jealous of others; and I'm always genuinely happy when good things happen for other people! Please show me where I am guilty of coveting." In a split second He showed me a picture of myself watching hair commercials on television as I envied the thick, long, gorgeous hair that everyone seemed to have, except me.

I began to realize that I did in fact have a problem with "hair envy," not only during television commercials but whenever I saw a person with thick, wavy beautiful hair...I wanted it! I didn't want theirs, but I wanted some just like theirs! My hair is baby fine, thin, straight, and boring! (A genetic trait I have inherited.) I saw clearly that I had become not only envious of beautiful hair, but obsessed with it!

Immediately I repented and asked God to forgive me and change me in that area. After that, whenever I became tempted to envy (complain in my mind), I would begin to thank God out loud for my own hair. "Thank You that I have hair!" I said, "And thank You for making it this color." (The color of my hair was the only thing I had ever liked about it.)

Before too long, I was no longer envious or coveting. Now, when I'm tempted to complain, I simply think about all the other things that God has blessed me with, and there are far too many to mention. God is good!

Like I said at the beginning: Envy has to go! *"For where envy and self-seeking exist, confusion and every evil thing are there"* (James 3:16).

You are special! You have everything you need in order to do what you have been called to do. Everybody needs to feel like "somebody"; but your self-worth, as Thomas Davidson said so well, "consists in what you are, and not in what you have; what you are will show in what you do."

Trust God. Repent for your past envy, and let Him take you into a wonderful world of peace, joy, and true fulfillment. *"My God shall supply all your need"* (Philippians 4:19).

Prayer for Contentment

Dear God,

Please deliver me from envy, jealousy, and covetousness. Forgive me for my past mistakes, and change me. Help me to see and appreciate the best in others and the best in myself.

Remind me often of all the many blessings You have given me. Help me to be satisfied with what I have as I continue to trust You to take me from strength to strength and from glory to glory. Amen.

Chapter Twelve

FORGIVENESS

Do I Have To?

Chapter Twelve

FORGIVENESS

Do I Have To?

Dear God,

I know that I am supposed to forgive everyone, but how

is that always possible? Some things that have happened

to me in the past are truly unforgivable.

Please tell me how to get past the pain and betrayal.

S ometimes it seems like an impossible request given
the gravity with which you were harmed. But still,
God insists that *"if you forgive men their trespasses,
your heavenly Father will also forgive you. But if you do not forgive men their trespasses, neither will your Father forgive your
trespasses"* (Matthew 6:14–15). God will never ask us to do

something that we are not able to do. Don't stop reading. There is help ahead!

Whatever happened to you cannot compare with what God has done for you. He sent His Son to die for all injustice and to purchase forgiveness for all of us—when none of us deserve it. He is very clear about the fact that, in order to receive forgiveness for our own faults, we must first forgive others for theirs. I don't know about you, but I need forgiveness every day.

Whatever has happened to you cannot compare with what God has done for you.

HOW DO I FORGIVE?

The best way to get rid of bitterness and unforgiveness is to simply give it to God. Tell Him honestly (since He already knows what you are thinking) that it's too hard and that you just can't do it on your own—in fact, that if the truth were to be known, you don't really want to forgive but you know that you must. He will help you from there.

Several years ago, a friend of mine was dealing with his own issue of unforgiveness. He had been stabbed in the back, the front, and on every side by people he had trusted, and it devastated him. As hard as he tried, he just couldn't seem to shake off the anger. A root of bitterness had begun to grow. One day as he was praying to God for help, God said, "Are you willing to forgive them and give it to Me?" My friend, surprised by his own answer, responded, "Lord, they hurt me so bad. I don't know if I'm willing." God then replied in His wonderful, loving way, "Are you willing that I should make you willing?"

All we have to do is be willing! He will do the rest! Our heavenly Father is so awesome, and so full of love for us, that He will truly do the work on our behalf if we will simply be obedient and let Him.

WHO ARE YOU HURTING?

My father and mother divorced when I was five years old. One summer afternoon, thirty years later, as I was talking with my mother, she began to share her feelings about my father. The pain and rejection she had experienced as a result of that divorce thirty years earlier had turned into a volcano of anger and bitterness. I listened to her voice become as that of a stranger's and watched her countenance fall and her lovely facial features distort. With each word she spoke, the volcano came closer and closer to erupting. I finally stopped her and said, "Mom! That was thirty years ago!"

"You don't know how he hurt me!" she fired back.

When you hold unforgiveness in your heart, you are the one who suffers.

"Let it go, Mom," I said. "He probably doesn't even remember it, and you continue to make yourself sick by holding on to the pain." I began to see clearly why she had been plagued with so many physical ailments throughout the years. That anger and unforgiveness had become like a cancer in her body, destroying her health, her youth, and her joy.

The bottom line is this: When you hold unforgiveness in your heart toward anyone, you are the one who will suffer the most. The person who hurt you may not even remember the incident. He is probably out somewhere enjoying himself,

completely ignorant of your pain. Your forgiveness is for you, not for him. Once you forgive him, you are free! When you are free, a root of bitterness cannot begin to grow inside of you. Unforgiveness can cause sickness, disease, and bitterness. It will also stop the flow of God's anointing in your life. If you want to go on with God, you've got to let go of past hurts and forgive.

True forgiveness always forgets.

"Well, I may forgive, but I'll never forget." How many times have you heard people say that? That is simply another way of saying, "I won't forgive." True forgiveness always forgets. When God forgives us, He remembers it no more. That also means that He will never bring it up again and use it against you, the way people do. *"As far as the east is from the west, so far has He removed our transgressions from us"* (Psalm 103:12). We need to be more like Him.

DIVINE JUSTICE

There was a king who wanted to settle accounts with his servants. When he had begun to settle accounts, one man was brought to him who owed him ten thousand talents. Since he was unable to pay that amount, the king commanded that he be sold, with his wife and children and all that he had, and that the payment be made. This servant fell down before the king saying, "Master have patience with me, and I will pay you all." The king was moved with compassion, released the man, and forgave his entire debt.

That same servant went out and found one of his own servants who owed him a much smaller debt. He took him by the throat and said, "Pay me what you owe me!" The man trembled, fell down at his feet, and begged him, saying, "Have

patience with me, and I will pay you all." He would not but instead threw the man in prison until he could pay the debt.

When his fellow servants saw what had been done, they were very upset and told the king what had taken place. The king then called the servant and said to him, "You wicked servant! I forgave you all that debt because you begged me. Should you not also have had compassion on you fellow servant, just as I had pity on you?"

The king was very angry and delivered the servant to the torturers until he should pay all that was due to him. (See Matthew 18:23–35.)

"So My heavenly Father also will do to you if each of you, from his heart, does not forgive his brother his trespasses" (verse 35).

This story always reminds me to practice the Golden Rule: "Do unto others as you would have others do unto you." (See Matthew 7:12.)

NO EXCUSES

One common mistake we often make in asking forgiveness from someone we have hurt is to give reasons or excuses for why we did what we did. We often try to justify ourselves to the wounded party. We say, "I'm sorry that I hurt you, but I was really having a bad day, and I just couldn't deal with anything else." That is asking someone to help us validate our own bad behavior. A true apology is asking forgiveness because we sincerely regret having hurt someone.

When you have hurt or wronged someone, it's no longer about you; it's about them. A simple and sincere "I'm so sorry. Please forgive me" is the most honest way to apologize. No "ifs," "ands," or "buts" allowed.

IT WORKS BOTH WAYS

When someone who has done you wrong comes back to you asking forgiveness, it is your job to accept it, forgive them, and forget about it. That means don't talk about it, don't gossip about it, and don't let anyone else pull you into conversation about it. It is over. It is finished. Move on!

God tells us in His Word that we are supposed to forgive our brother not just seven times but rather seventy times seven. In other words, don't keep score. Stop counting how many times others have hurt you. Forgive them, and again, move on.

The ultimate example of forgiveness, in my opinion, was when Jesus, nailed to the cross and near death, looked down at his persecutors and said, *"Father, forgive them, for they know not what they do"* (Luke 23:34 KJV). Surely none of us will ever have to forgive as much as He did.

Prayer for a Forgiving Spirit

Dear God,

Please forgive me for not forgiving _____. I realize that in order to be free, I am going to have to forgive _____ and let go of the past. I can't do it alone; please help me. Remind me of all the times You forgave me when I didn't deserve it, and help me to do the same.

God, if I'm not willing, please make me willing. I want to be right in Your sight. I want to go on with the wonderful life You have prepared for me. Thank You for Your love. Help me to share that love with others. Amen.

Chapter Thirteen

SUCCESS

You Were Born for It!

SUCCESS

You Were Born for It!

Dear God,

How can I become successful? All around me I see people succeeding and reaching their goals while I stand on the sidelines and watch. I work hard, but I just never seem to go anywhere. What am I doing wrong?

Working hard is not the key to success (although success will involve hard work). Working smart is the key to success. But first of all, what is it that you want?

Before you can become successful, you must define success. Success means different things to different people. For some people, the ultimate success means having a loving, working relationship, while for others it involves the amount

of money in their bank accounts. Athletes often look at success from the vantage point of winning tournaments, races, or competitions. Artists may view success as finishing a novel or a painting, or winning an Oscar, an Emmy, or a Grammy. Parents often feel successful if their children are healthy and happy. So the first question to answer is, "What does success mean to you?"

What does success mean to you?

One of the traps you want to avoid in finding success is blaming your lack of it on your circumstances. For example, many people think, "If I only had more money, I'd be happier," "If I only had a different husband," "If I could just have more time to myself," "If I had a better job, bigger house, nicer car...." If you give your circumstances the power to control you, they will, and you will never be successful. One of the steps to success is learning how to look past the circumstances while keeping your eyes on the desired goal. Jesus was surely the most successful man who ever lived because *"for the joy that was set before Him* [He] *endured the cross"* (Hebrews 12:2). In other words, He wasn't looking at His circumstances, which I think we would all agree, were not looking good as He climbed the hill to be nailed to the cross. But He wasn't looking at the cross. He was focused on the prize, *"the joy that was set before him,"* the resurrection and salvation of the world.

To become a success you must stop reacting to things around you. It's not what's "out there" that needs to change. It's what's inside of you that must change in order to bring you the success you desire.

Begin to act as the star in your drama called life. Go ahead; cast yourself in the leading role. You are also the producer

and director. Now, what would you like to create? Most successful people are dreamers; ordinary people who dare to do extraordinary things. (Read about Abraham Lincoln in chapter two, *Faith*; or Mother Teresa in chapter six, *Love*.)

GET THE PICTURE

Most people never become successful because they don't even know what they really want. Successful people always have a dream or a vision. They also have a passion about that vision. They have a determination to succeed, whatever the cost. In other words, they are willing to pay the price. Many, however, stop right there. They may have an idea or a dream, but they haven't developed the character and self-discipline it will take to launch them into the success they desire. So they sit on the sidelines, hoping that maybe someday things will be different. They won't.

Successful people have a vision. They also have passion about that vision.

Nothing will change in our lives until we change. The definition of insanity is doing the same thing over and over and expecting different results. Two plus two will always equal four, no matter how many times you do the math. Are you ready? Do you really want to change your life and become more successful? And are you willing to pay the price?

So, again I ask, what do you want? What is success to you? What do you most enjoy doing? That is a good indication of where your greatest success will lie. What are your personal values? Will your desire for success compromise those values? In other words, although you may want to earn more money, will your relationships with your family suffer as a result? If

so, which is really more important to you? Is there perhaps a way that you could have both?

In building a house, any good contractor knows that, before he begins to pound nails and put up the dry wall, he first needs blueprints to show him what the house will potentially look like. You need a new set of blueprints. It is vital to your success that you construct a clear picture of what you want to build. Make that image as detailed as possible. *"Write the vision and make it plain on tablets, that he may run who reads it"* (Habakkuk 2:2). Who is *"he"*? *"He"* is you.

When God asked Noah to build an ark, he gave Noah specific instructions and dimensions. He told Noah to make the ark out of gopher wood and then went on to say, *"And this is how you shall make it: The length of the ark shall be three hundred cubits, its width fifty cubits, and its height thirty cubits"* (Genesis 6:15). God had given him blueprints, and Noah built the ark exactly as God directed, insuring success for himself and his family during the flood.

VISION VERSUS VICTORY

Many of us have a vision of losing weight and getting into great shape; but only those who are willing to pay the price of proper diet and exercise will ever achieve that goal. Turning your vision into victory will require discipline. "Ouch! Did she have to use the 'D' word?" Yes, I did. No discipline means no success.

Turning your vision into victory
will require discipline.

So once you have your blueprints, make a promise to yourself that you will continue the work until it is finished.

Develop a work ethic and keep it. Daily discipline will keep you strong through the end of the race. Many people drop out at the eleventh hour, not realizing how close they are to success. *"For you have need of endurance, so that after you have done the will of God, you may receive the promise"* (Hebrews 10:36). The *"will of God"* is that you succeed! How do I know that? *"I pray that you may prosper in all things"* (3 John 2). Don't ever give up! Keep the vision continually before your eyes. Live in it, walk in it, and even sleep in it until it becomes more real than the circumstances and things that surround you.

It took Noah one hundred and twenty years to build the ark. You know there were many times he probably felt like giving up. There had never been rain on the earth before, and everyone was laughing at him. Talk about stepping out in faith and taking a risk! But Noah didn't quit or give up; he persevered. And because he did, he and his family were the only people on the earth who succeeded at staying alive.

How about Rocky? How many times did we watch him run up those stairs and through the streets of Philadelphia in the early morning hours? Remember how he came home each day so exhausted and bruised after punching those huge slabs of meat hanging in the cooler? Before he became the champ, he beat his body into submission and disciplined himself to a regimen required for the success he desired.

The reason Nehemiah was able to rebuild the wall was because *"the people had a mind to work"* (Nehemiah 4:6). Success doesn't come without work.

Academy-award-winning actress Meryl Streep recently shared in a television interview that, in the beginning of her career, she spent over five years in New York trying to find an agent. Nobody wanted her! Good thing she didn't give up!

The movie script for *Gone with the Wind* spent nearly ten years sitting on bookshelves as one studio after another passed on the project. It eventually became one of the greatest and most successful movies ever made.

Producer Gloria Monty accepted the huge challenge of taking over the show *General Hospital* for ABC when it was at the bottom of the ratings. She had a vision, took many risks (one of whom was me), worked hard, and catapulted *General Hospital* to the top of the charts within one year. Her success was unprecedented. Most everyone today remembers Luke and Laura, their wedding, and the cover of *Newsweek*. I will always be grateful to her for giving me my first big break in acting.

CREATE ORDER!

I have never met a successful man or woman who wasn't organized. Clutter creates confusion. In Washington, D.C., in the Library of Congress, there are five words written on the ceiling: "Order is Heaven's first law."

If you don't take the practical steps required for success, you're living in a dream.

You can tell yourself all day long that you are going to be successful. You can shout it from the highest mountain and believe it with your whole heart; but if you don't take the practical steps required to change your life so that you can actually be more successful, then you're just living in a dream. Hope sits on a chair and wishes. Faith gets up and acts. Go ahead! Take control of your life! Isn't it time?

If you don't have a daily planner, get one and use it. Making a daily plan the night before has helped me stay effective and

organized more than anything else. When you write things down, you no longer have the excuse of forgetting. Learning to prioritize is also important. When you make your list, decide which things must be done today and which things could actually wait until later. You can work hard long hours and still not be effective and successful at achieving your goals if your priorities are messed up. Order is imperative.

Returning phone calls promptly is another sign of a successful man or woman. I will never forget a man by the name of Randy. Many years ago I was in a difficult financial position, and a business associate gave me Randy's phone number. I called Randy's office one day to see if he might be able to help me get a car loan. Since I had never met the man, I was very impressed when he returned my phone call within the hour, saying that he would indeed be happy to help me, which he did very professionally and graciously. I was far more impressed however, when I discovered the next day that he was the president of the bank! "Now I see why he's the president," I said to myself. "He returns phone calls, and he is prompt in his business." *Do you see a man who excels in his work* [is prompt in his business]? *He will stand before kings; he will not stand before unknown men*" (Proverbs 22:29). In other words, he will be successful. Like cream, he will rise to the top.

YOUR ATTITUDE WILL CREATE YOUR ALTITUDE

There are many things in life that we cannot control, like earthquakes, tornadoes, the stock market, and our national debt, but we can make the choice to control our lives and our emotions. We can choose to be positive rather than negative, to see the proverbial glass half full instead of half empty.

Everyone loves to be around successful, positive, encouraging people. Nobody likes a whiner. Success does not come by chance, but by choice. It is not something to be waited on, but pursued!

Each morning when I wake up, the first words out of my mouth are, *"This is the day the LORD has made; we will rejoice and be glad in it"* (Psalm 118:24)! I make a choice; I "will" to rejoice. I don't allow myself time enough to wake up and see how I feel because feelings change. Feelings are deceptive. If I went by my feelings, I'd roll over and go back to sleep. We must strengthen our will and crucify our flesh if we are going to be successful.

A joyful positive attitude is imperative to success.

Right now, right where you are, begin to smile. I dare you. If you are brave enough to accept this challenge, you will find that, somewhere between five and ten seconds, you will begin to feel happier. You can use this trick throughout your day to keep your spirits high and your enemies confused.

Last but not least, don't let your past failures determine your future success! The past is over; that's why we call it the "passed." A certain cartoonist once said, "All our dreams can come true if we have the courage to pursue them." He started out broke, with only a dream and a sketch of a little mouse. Now the whole world has heard of Walt Disney and his friend, Mickey Mouse.

Remember, success is not a destination, but a journey. Enjoy the trip! And after you have made the decision to go for the gold, and you've disciplined yourself, created a positive attitude, and put order in your life, then and only then, take time to pat yourself on the back. You deserve it. A joyful, positive attitude is imperative to success. Encourage yourself continually. And, again, remember, it's all about the journey.

Prayer for Success

Dear God,

Please give me the vision, the courage, and the stamina to create success in my life. I want to excel at those things You have called me and given me the talent to do.

Help me to not be afraid. Help me to find the freedom inherent in discipline. Help me to always remember that with You, all things are possible! Amen.

Chapter Fourteen

GRACE

Where Can I Find Some?

Chapter Fourteen

GRACE

Where Can I Find Some?

Dear God,

How come some Christians don't always act, well, Christian? Aren't they supposed to be filled with God's love? It seems like most of the Christians I know go to church on Sunday and then forget everything they hear as soon as they leave their pew. I'm trying hard to be a good person, but, why? Maybe I don't need to try so hard either.

Hurting people run to churches hoping for answers, forgiveness, and grace but too often find just the opposite: criticism, gossip, and slander. "*These things*

142

ought not to be so" (James 3:10). Unfortunately, this assessment of many churches today is accurate. We embrace the theology of grace but we don't live it.

The great English writer C. S. Lewis caught a glimpse of grace one day as he received a revelation while repeating the Apostle's Creed: "I believe in the forgiveness of sins." He later went on to explain Christianity this way: "To be a Christian means to forgive the inexcusable, because God has forgiven the inexcusable in you." Yet, sadly, this element of basic Christianity is profoundly missing from most churches and in most Christians. The question is, What can we do to help change it?

IT STARTS WITH ME

Someone once said, "If it is to be, it begins with me." Someone else put it another way, "The buck stops here!" Are you willing to be the first one on your block, in your church, or at your office to turn on the flow of the fountain of grace?

Grace means unmerited favor—favor we don't deserve. It is easy to give grace to a person who is treating you well, but to show the same grace to one who has stabbed you in the back and slandered your good name is a bit more difficult. That kind of grace can only be given with the help of God.

> "God, please forgive us, and help us to change."

Christianity's principle, "Hate the sin but love the sinner," is far more easily preached than practiced. Although we embrace it in theory, we often fall short in execution. When I first gave my life to the Lord, I was ecstatic about the fact that I was now on the winning team! I would weep continually at the realization of God's great mercy and grace. His love

overshadowed everything else in my life, and I was so grateful that He hadn't left me behind. I assumed that everyone else in His church body felt the same way. How wonderful it was to be part of such a loving, caring, harmonious family!

Unfortunately, my naïveté was soon squelched. Gossip began to fly. Criticism crawled through the cracks. Condemnation and judgment emanated even from the pulpit! What was happening? My beautiful dream was becoming a nightmare. I was beyond disappointed; I was devastated. "God, this is wrong!" I would cry out. "We are supposed to be kind and forgiving like You!" My heart began to break, not for myself, not even for the church, but for God, who had given so much and been given so little in return. "How this must hurt Him," I thought. "God, please forgive us, and help us to change," I prayed. "Help us to remember that we are all Your children! Help us to knock down the walls that separate us from one another. Surely there are no denominations in heaven." God was silent. I think He was crying too.

SHEEP BEATERS

I'm not sure if this paragraph will ever make it to press, but I feel obligated to make mention of the fact that there are some leaders today who are beating the sheep instead of loving, restoring, teaching, and nurturing them. God is not pleased with this behavior. Your job as a leader is to care for God's children like the Good Shepherd did.

Just because you're anointed does not give you the right to mistreat those God has put under your care. Just because you sit in the seat of authority does not give you God's blessing to overwork, manipulate, and control the sheep using the name of the Lord. They may serve you for a season because you've

convinced them that they should. But when they end up over-worked, underpaid, and confused, feeling ripped off, abused, and abandoned, they will leave. Many of them will backslide and never return to a church. And you will be held account-able to God Himself. Every child is precious in His sight!

Take your eyes off the person who hurt you and put them back on the Lord.

If you are someone who has been mistreated by ministry, I ask your forgiveness on behalf of the body of Christ. You are important, and we need you. I pray that you will take your eyes off the person or persons who hurt you and put them back on the Lord. He will help you to forgive, even though they don't deserve it (see chapter 12, *Forgiveness*), and will cover you once more with His unfathomable love and grace. Men may let you down, but God will never fail you. Let Him love you again!

WORLD GRACE

My credit card contracts have what they call a "grace period," which means that if I don't pay the amount due by the agreed upon due date, they will give me an extra few days to pay without charging me a penalty. Blockbuster gave me over an hour of "grace time" just the other day when I returned a movie. Even car rental agencies will give you an hour or two "grace time" in returning their cars. The world has caught on to the power of grace. Everyone wants grace! Grace is good!

Recently I called a doctor's office regarding a bill they kept sending me. My records showed that I had already paid them what I owed. "You had a missed appointment back in February," said the assistant. "I don't remember ever missing

an appointment," I replied. She asked me to check my day timer to see if I had any record of the appointment. When I called her back to tell her that I did not have any doctors' appointments written on my calendar for that month, I asked her if she would please give me some grace in this situation. She returned my call the following day saying that she had erased the charge. Once again, there was grace. Thank you, Marilyn.

My sister, Rae, is one of the most generous people I have ever met. She gives grace to everyone she meets, whether it's a struggling homeless person, the president of a successful corporation, or the neighborhood stray cat. She is a living example of grace, giving unmerited favor and love to all who cross her path.

As members of the body of Christ we ought to be more like God.

Every day, our lives should reflect more love toward others than the day before. We ought to be more compassionate, more forgiving, more like God. Wouldn't it be wonderful if the members of the body of Christ actually started living like they were part of the same body?

MAKE GRACE YOUR CALLING CARD

Wouldn't you like to be known as a person of grace? Wouldn't it be nice to have people continually tell others about how loving, kind, and encouraging you are? More importantly, wouldn't it be awesome to daily come before God and hear Him say to you, "I am well pleased"? Those are the words God spoke to Jesus as He was baptized in the Jordan River; and God's purpose for us is that we *"be conformed to the image*

of His Son" (Romans 8:29). So, since God spoke those words to Jesus, He wants to also speak those same words to us.

The answer is so simple: *"Love one another"* as He has asked us to (John 13:34). And if we fail, at least we have tried. Even then, we have His promise that *"My grace is sufficient for you"* (2 Corinthians 12:9). He will be there to pick us up, brush us off, and help us start again. How amazing is His grace!

The grace God showed the world by sending His Son is beyond what we, as mere mortals, are able to demonstrate; but the grace to love others as ourselves, the grace to forgive as He has forgiven us, and the grace to place another's needs before our own are all examples of the grace that we are capable of giving. Bake a cake for someone, forgive a debt, or let someone have the parking place you were headed for. Grace is love in action.

Prayer for Grace

Dear God,

Please fill me with Your grace, and help me to pass it on to others. Forgive me for the times I was critical instead of compassionate. Help me to see others through Your eyes so that I won't be so quick to judge them; and remind me to look in the mirror when I am tempted to point my finger.

God, please help us to remember that we are all Your children and that You love each one of us. Help us to tear down the racial and denominational walls that tend to separate instead of unify; for there is power in unity, while a house divided against itself cannot stand.

Teach us, Lord, to be more like You. Amen.

CONCLUSION

CONCLUSION

I t is my hope and prayer that, as you have read this book and found yourself hiding among some of the pages, you have been encouraged, inspired, and empowered to rise above your problems and situations by taking them to God and allowing Him to give you instruction, revelation, and peace.

I want to challenge you to pray more because I know that prayer works. Prayer changes things, and you would not have read this book unless you had some things in your life that needed changing. In the back of this book, you will find a special reminder made just for you. Remove the card and frame it, hang it, or put it on your refrigerator. Then, after you have prayed and changed your situation, write to me with your results.

Let me share with you just a few changes that prayer has made in my own life:

- Years ago my son was diagnosed with an incurable disease. The doctors finally gave up, saying there was nothing more they could do. It was the lowest point in my life. God then spoke to my friend and me instructing us to pray and fast for

150

five days; He wanted to heal my son. We did as He requested, and on the fifth day my son was miraculously healed. Prayer changes things!

- In 1994 I found a lump in my breast. I said, "No!" The doctors said "cancer." But God said, "Don't sign for it. Just trust Me." So I trusted Him, prayed His Word over my situation continually, and within weeks the lump was completely gone, never to return again. The doctors were perplexed, and God was glorified. Faith mixed with prayer changed things.

- Gina, a member of our women's prayer group, was pregnant when she developed severe pneumonia. Her temperature rose to 105 degrees. We prayed and asked God to heal her. Within hours the fever was gone and her lungs, completely cleared. The doctors were amazed and had no explanation. Again, prayer had changed things.

- Kim, another member of our prayer group, needed $100,000 for the closing of a film project she was working on. Time had grown short, and she needed a miracle. We agreed in prayer, asking God to move on her behalf, reminding Him that His Word promised that "with God nothing is impossible." Within two days the entire amount was provided from an unexpected source. Our prayers, once again, had changed things.

- David, the head of a television studio here in California, hadn't slept for more than two hours a night for many years due to tormenting spirits and health problems. We prayed for him one

151

night, bound the tormenting spirits, and asked God to "give His beloved sleep" according to His Word. The next morning David's wife called me with joyful tears of thanksgiving. David had slept that night for more than eight hours straight; she could not remember the last time that had happened. You know what I'm going to say next.... Prayer changes things!

I hope that these words have encouraged you to pray more. Prayer is simply talking to God. He loves to hear your voice. He is faithful. And you are the apple of His eye!

"Onward!" my friends,

God loves you!

Gail

P.S. Please feel free to contact us.

We would love to hear your comments, questions, or prayer requests.

Women in Entertainment

8033 Sunset Blvd., Suite 221

Hollywood, CA 90046

Or on the web at www.womeninentertainment.org

Or by phone at (818)415-4880

ABOUT THE AUTHOR
Gail Ramsey

ABOUT THE AUTHOR

Gail Ramsey is known to many as "Susan Moore," the popular character she played on ABC's *General Hospital* for five years. Gail also starred as "Linda Chambers" on the *Mike Hammer Show*, "Laura McCallum" on NBC's *Generations*, and can currently be seen in reruns of the NBC comedy, *California Dreams*.

Gail has used her celebrity status both as an actress and an athlete, winning many trophies in golf (The Crosby and Frank Sinatra tournaments), tennis (the Monte Carlo and Michael Landon tournaments), and skiing events in Aspen, Vail, and Jackson Hole.

On New Year's Eve of 1990, Gail's life took a radical turn. She became a Christian. Three years later Gail took a sabbatical from Hollywood and attended Bible college. After graduation Gail was ordained and began traveling from churches to prisons and to the deepest interiors of Africa. She teaches, preaches, and encourages powerfully through television, radio, and the pulpit.

Gail currently resides in Southern California and continues to write her weekly newspaper column of nine years, *Dear God!* which combines biblical principles with humorous Hollywood antics, encouraging the reader to receive the love and forgiveness of his Maker, and to live life as "more than a

conqueror"! *Dear God!* is also alive internationally on the air-waves via radio.

Still very active in the entertainment arena, Gail has recently been cast in the upcoming feature film *Valentine* and is in preproduction for *Healthy in Hollywood*, a television series she created and is producing with her partner, a former network president. "The purpose of *Healthy in Hollywood*," says Gail, "is to reclaim the airwaves for family viewing by raising the moral standard of current television programming."

Gail is the founder of "Women in Entertainment," a ministry committed to empowering women of integrity to triumph in the entertainment business. She leads a bimonthly Bible study/prayer meeting by the same name, comprised of key women in Hollywood, and teaches a weekly Bible study open to both men and women in the business. Gail is committed to empowering people to be all that God created them to be. "It's the compassion of Jesus, coupled with holy boldness, that gets the job done," says Gail. "We must be shining examples of a victorious and risen Christ! If people can see the joy of the Lord and the power of the Holy Spirit flowing through us and view us as more than conquerors, then the seduction of the world won't seem so inviting."

For more information about Gail Ramsey or Women in Entertainment,

Write to:

Women in Entertainment
8033 Sunset Blvd., Suite 221
Hollywood, CA 90046

Website: www.womeninentertainment.org

Phone: (818)415-4880

Journal

Journal

Journal

_____
_____
_____
_____
_____
_____
_____
_____
_____
_____
_____
_____
_____
_____
_____
_____
_____
_____
_____
_____
_____
_____
_____
_____
_____

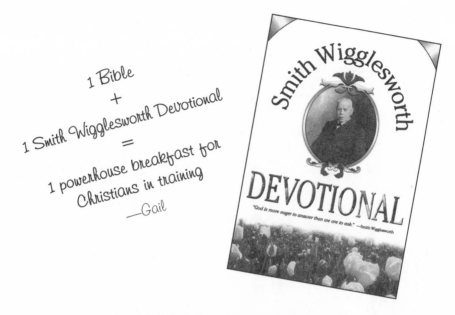

1 Bible
+
1 Smith Wigglesworth Devotional
=
1 powerhouse breakfast for
Christians in training
—Gail

Smith Wigglesworth Devotional
Smith Wigglesworth

"This book is not for wimps! Light years beyond religious rhetoric, through the galaxy of timeless wisdom, Smith Wigglesworth catapults you into the fourth dimension where all things are not only possible, but expected. Here is a devotional experience that will rock your world, destroy your religious ideas, and open your eyes to the bottom-line truth of Jesus Christ. If you want to move past the daily norm of religious prayers into the powerful presence and essence of Christ, this book is for you!

"Smith Wigglesworth is truly one of my greatest heroes."
—Gail Ramsey

ISBN: 0-88368-574-4 • Trade • 560 pages

WHITAKER
HOUSE

proclaiming the power of the Gospel through the written word
visit our website at www.whitakerhouse.com